# FREE AT LAST:

## *A Disciple's Journey*

David Louis Norris Jr.

ISBN: 978-0-9891973-6-6

# Acknowledgments

*My sincere appreciation to*

*Kelly Herndon and Katie Davis*

*for their help outlining and editing this book.*

# CONTENTS

# Preface

I have not done anything worthy of writing a book that people should read except give my life to the Lord and live for Him. Accepting Jesus is the only honorable thing I have ever done. I am not publishing this book to glorify sin or myself. I am *"Free at Last"* because I finally understand how ugly I am on a daily basis, and it is *"Not I, But Christ"*[1] who is worthy to be proclaimed. While preparing a rough manuscript several years ago, it dawned on me that overcoming the challenges of this journey was remarkable, but the fact still remains, I didn't overcome those challenge on my own.

This insight brought awareness that what Christ has done in me, He has done and will do in countless others like me. So what makes my story book-worthy? This was a profound and humbling question that I needed to answer at the time I first started writing my disciple's journey.

The first time I began my story, I was so easily puffed up, and as a result, I found myself dying to my own selfish ambitions. Christ made it clear to me that at that point of the journey; my motives were impure and full of selfish ambition. At that revelation I placed my unfinished manuscript on the shelf with the thought, *"Who am I and what is my life that people should want to hear from me?"* I am nothing and my life is nothing unless my motives are to proclaim Christ.

So why did I dust this manuscript off and pick something back up that Christ asked me to lie down for a season? I have counted the cost, picked up the cross, and followed Jesus as a disciple. The person I have become and the life I have left behind has significant meaning

---

[1] Motto taken in 2011 and adopted on the wall of my office from Galatians 2:20 "I have been crucified with Christ and I no longer live, but Christ lives in me...NIV"

to my daughter, Breanna. I also hope my daughter Kaylin will forgive me and turn to Christ so that our relationship can be restored.

On January 18, 2014 I received a text from Breanna that said *"So are you ever going to get your book published? You need to!!!"* Breanna is my daughter from a previous marriage before Christ. We gained custody of Breanna and delivered her out of a lifestyle similar to what God brought us out of. She was a great student and volleyball player. At the age of fourteen, she would fast with me for three day intervals denying her flesh of everything but water. Breanna is my prodigal daughter, but I look out over the horizon and hope to one day see her coming home.

This is why I will share my life and the deep seeded truths of *"A Disciple's Journey."* My aim is that through Jesus Christ and the release of this writing she comes home. If nothing else occurs then I am content. O how I pray that this story will set her free in Jesus name.

*Picture of Breanna in the summer of 2009*

Happy Birthday Dad!!
It hasn't been a great
year for us, but it has been a
great year for you! You've accomplish
ed your biggest dream - literally.
I can't be anything but proud of
you. Your a great dad and you've been
nothing but good to me and I've
repayed you with anger, bitterness,
and disrespect. I'm very sorry for all
the cruel things I've done to you,
said to or about you and everything
else. I hope that we can make
this an even better year for us
and move forward a little bit.
I love you.
♡ -Breanna

*Letter from Breanna written around April 13th 2013*

# Introduction

My name is David Norris and I was born in Bloomington, Indiana but raised just south in Bedford. You are going to read a lot about my life over the next seven chapters; however, before we begin I want to give you a very brief overview of who I am and who I represent. First, I want to emphasize that I have not always been an upright and noble man that lives his life for God first and others second. In my previous life before Christ, I took all that I could get from anyone that I could get it from. I cared about no one and loved only myself. I will begin this portion of the story by introducing the family that I now represent through the saving power and undeserving grace of the Lord Jesus Christ.

I have been married to my wife, Joy, for 15 years, six of which were without Christ. We are a blended family where she brought two children, Cody and Shannon, into the marriage. I brought two daughters, Kaylin and Breanna, with me as well by two separate women. We have one son between us named Caleb.

I was released from jail in 1998 and met Joy towards the end of that same year. We married on December 17, 1999 and by 2005 I had crossed every line I had established for myself. I had no self-worth. I was an alcoholic, dope-dealing, pill-popping heroin addict. My businesses were in utter ruin and failure and I had stolen over $100,000 from my business partner and best friend. I had no way of paying him back. So, behind the counter in a hydroponic shop called *"Organics Plus"* I cried out to Jesus to save me, and He met me where I was and radically changed my life.

The first two years of walking with the Lord was everything He said it would be. The third year of walking with the Lord was more than I could have ever asked for. We became members of Crossroads Community Church in 2007, and I was voted to the position of Chaplin at Oakland City University in 2008. In 2009 I graduated with an Associate of Arts in Religion. In the summer of 2009 we were not sure what God had next, so I began to pray. I asked God for three things as our family followed Him. One, provide for my family. Two, allow me to work in the ministry and three, allow me to continue my education.

To this day God has come through and is still answering these requests. My family has never had to go begging for bread, and since that time, I have had many opportunities to work in different types of ministries. I am currently the Founder and Director of an in-house discipleship ministry, Heaven Nevaeh Healing Center located in Judah, Indiana that is involved in radically changing lives through our Lord Jesus Christ. I earned my Bachelors of Science in Religion from Liberty University (LU) in 2011 and recently completed the requirements for my Masters of Arts in Theological Studies degree from LU in the spring of 2014.

Where we are going from here is unknown. The Lord has revealed bits and pieces of our future and what it looks like. At the very least, we know we are called to be disciples with servants' hearts, and that is our future. Whatever successes come our way will be for the benefit of others, and I pray that is always our heart's desire as we follow Christ on this disciple's journey.

*[Picture of Organics Plus on next page.]*

Behind the counter of *'Organics Plus'*
where I was redeemed on November 1, 2005

# -1-

# From Death to Life

## *What Satan meant for evil the Lord meant for good.*

*"Some became fools through their rebellious ways and suffered affliction because of their iniquities. They loathed all food and drew near the gates of death. Then they cried to the LORD in their trouble, and he saved them from their distress. He sent forth his word and healed them; he rescued them from the grave. Let them give thanks to the LORD for his unfailing love and his wonderful deeds for men. Let them sacrifice thank offerings and tell of his works with songs of joy".*

Psalm 107: 17-22NIV

I was born on April 13, 1969 at 10:29 a.m. I was a sick baby and the facts of my early years may carry more weight coming from the voice of my mother, Rosann Norris.

["As the mother of David Norris Jr. I have found myself doing some pretty stupid things, and have come to realize that I'm not any more perfect than the next person. God knew we would do stupid things in this life, that's why he provided a Savior, so we would have the opportunity to repent and move on, trying every day to do better than the last.

Since I have realized my own weaknesses and my own stupidity, I have found it easier to live by the scripture found in the Holy Bible *"Judge not, that ye be not judged. For with what judgment ye judge, ye shall be judged; and with what measure ye mete, it shall be measured to you again"* (Matthew 7:1-2 KJV). I try not to judge the past of other people or their present mistakes because I know how merciful my Heavenly Father and Jesus Christ has been toward me, and how repentance has played a big part in my life. We can't truly know another person's heart, so I leave the judgment to God and pray for myself and others who continually struggle to stay on the right path.

There comes a time in all of our lives when we come to know Satan personally, and hopefully, before it is too late, realize the scripture that says *"he can fool even the very elect"*[2] is very true. So with that said, I will focus on the happiness and joy David has brought to his dad and me.

As I reflect on David's early years, my mind goes back to the time when his dad, David Sr., and I were growing up. David Sr. and I were both from a family of eight children. When David Sr. was 13 he became not only the son of Delbert and Mae Norris, but one of five sons and three daughters. The respect and responsibility he gave to his mother would continue for the next 40 years until her death at 85 years of age.

David Sr.'s family life was very simple, as was mine. My dad was strict and my mother was passive. I think David Sr.'s parents were just the opposite, but then I never had the opportunity to know his dad. His mother needed to be strict since she was a single mother.

---

[2] Paraphrase of Matthew 24:24 KJV

Neither of us had much material possessions, nor did we expect any more than a roof over our heads and food to eat. We weren't expected to, but took pride in working as teenagers and buying our own cloths. We were happy children with no bad habits, and enough respect and fear of our parents to stay out of trouble. Neither of our families were what you would call affectionate toward one another, verbally or physically. We just knew love and what it meant to be there for one another. Family was the most important thing to both of us. Friends had their place in our lives, but family was our number one focus, so we spent a lot of our spare time with our extended families.

When David Sr. and I met, he had been jilted by his fiancé, and I had been forgotten by my boyfriend who had gone off to the military. Even though both of us were encouraged to return to our previous relationships, we were comfortable in the relationship we had built together. And as I reflect on the 32 years we had together, I have to say it was a match made in heaven. You never saw two people as happy or more in love than we were.

David Sr. was raised Catholic and I was a Mormon, we both believed in pro-creation, so within a month of marriage, we were expecting our first child. David Norris Jr. made our love for one another blossom. To see physically, laying in our arms, a person that through our love for one another we had created was the most awesome thing we had ever experienced. It's amazing the powerful love you feel when you bring a life into the world that came from love.

We never once thought of all the material things we would give this child. Things weren't a part of our vocabulary because of the way we were raised. However, we wanted nothing but a good life for this child of ours. That meant we would teach him correct principles, spend time with him, and support him in all of his endeavors. David Sr. and I soon committed our life to serve in the Mormon Church.

One strong principle we aimed to teach our children was what our Mormon religion referred to as the *"Word of Wisdom."* That wine and strong drinks are not good except for offering up our sacraments before God, and then it should be pure of the grape of the vine, of your own make. That strong drink is not for the belly, but for the washing of our bodies. We taught that tobacco was not for the body, neither for the belly, and is not good for man, but is an herb for bruises and all sick cattle. We taught that hot drinks are not for the belly, interpreted to be coffee and tea. Through the years, I've discredited myself, as well as my late husband for not being an effective teacher; however, as life goes on I have seen that our teaching did have some effect.

*David Sr. & Rosann Norris with Davy in 1969*

David Jr., Davy, as we called him was a pleasant child (once I realized he needed more to eat). Even at 21 I wasn't the smartest mother. He sure had a rough start with his two dumb parents. The first four months were a nightmare, so I found it easier to take him to a babysitter and go back to work early. This would be one of my biggest regrets, and I think it may have kept him from attaching to us like he should have.

When Davy was 18-months old, I went to pick him up at the babysitter's house, and she informed me that he just laid around all day, which was unusual. I took him to the doctor and they suspected appendicitis. After some x-rays and examinations, appendicitis was ruled out and exploratory surgery was necessary.

The result was shocking. Our baby, our life's joy was given two days to live. He was diagnosed with viral hepatitis that was not treatable. Davy was anointed with oil and given a blessing of healing. The next day he was moved from intensive care to the regular patient floor. The doctors were in awe, saying that he had to have had a guardian angel watching over him. I believe this was the first miracle Davy would experience in his lifetime as he has related to me that he should be dead today.

As Davy continued to improve, I told his dad I would be quitting work to stay home with our baby, and he didn't argue with that. The next four years were wonderful with me being home. We had so little money, but we were happy.

A year later we added a daughter, Kim, to our little family. Before Kim turned three, I decided to go back to work so we could build a house. My job lasted for two years before I was permanently laid off. This was the best thing that ever happened because we began to notice the influence other children were having on our children. Nevertheless, we would learn later in life that living our children's lives for them was not going to happen.

We were so naïve to so many things that we were blinded by the obvious. We didn't realize that the things that our children would be up against would happen in a million years. We thought that if we raised them as good as but just a little better than we were raised, we would have this perfect family. With a love like ours, how could we fail? It wasn't going to happen that easily, though.

Davy had two bouts with pneumonia, and by the time he was six we learned he needed to have open heart surgery because of a heart murmur, which caused his problem, and could, in later years, cause an enlarged heart. I was able to be at Riley hospital with him for his duration there. We didn't have much money, so I ate a lot of pop tarts, and slept in a hard rocking chair, but I was happy that I could be there with him.

The day before his surgery someone came in and explained to him what they would be doing to prepare him for surgery so he would be comfortable with it. We really thought he was okay with everything. He always acted like a tough kid who wasn't afraid of anything.

The next morning, upon rising from bed, he went into the bathroom. After what seemed like an eternity, I went in to check on him. He looked at me with great fear and burst into tears and admitted that he was scared. I thought my heart would burst. I held him until he calmed down and they gave him an anesthetic to make him sleep.

We could only visit Davy for 15 minutes every hour up until 8:00 p.m. so the days were long and boring for me. David Sr. would come up on the weekend and keep me company. Memorial Day weekend we were invited to spend the night in a real bed at the home of Davy's Aunt Diane. We took advantage of it. However, the next morning leaving what we thought was early enough to arrive at the hospital for our first visit with Davy became a race through the Indianapolis 500 traffic. We pulled in just in time for me to hop out, while David Sr. parked the car. Being away from the hospital all night was one thing, but not being there first thing in the morning for Davy was unbearable to us. Every breath we breathed was for him and our daughter.

Davy was a pleasant child, so it wasn't surprising that he never complained of pain after his surgery. However, he and I were sitting one day watching *"The Three Stooges"* and he got to laughing so hard, he pulled his incision apart. I had to take him away from the TV so he wouldn't laugh. From that point on he never again had to be admitted to the hospital.

Our Heavenly Father has a plan for all of us, and we felt strongly that God had a special plan for our son, but we don't believe he had to go through all he put himself through to get there; he decided on his own to take the long way around.

Davy was a quiet, obedient child, always wanting to help around the house. I remember one Saturday morning at a very young age, he got out of bed, came running in our room and said, *"I cook breakfast."* We said, *"Okay."* He ran into the kitchen, ran back and asked, "You want toast?" *"Yes,"* we said. He ran into the kitchen, came back and said, *"You want egg?"* Again we said yes. He ran back into the kitchen, opened up the cabinet, reached for the skillet, and dropped it on his toe.

Another night, at age two, he switched the light on in the middle of the night to use the bathroom. I was so impressed that he could train himself to do that so young. I remember thinking how smart he must be.

I remember David Sr. and me walking through the mall with Davy running ahead of us. I can still see him with his blonde hair, his sparkling white baby shoes, snow white socks and white shorts against his tanned legs, and an olive green shirt. He was the most handsome toddler. I was so proud when an old classmate approached us so I could show him off. By this time, we thought we had not only the smartest kid around, but the cutest.

Davy thrived in sports, especially basketball. We were there for him come hell or high water with pride and our last penny to get in. I remember one night when he hit the winning basket in high school. He jumped, turned, and shot all in one motion. That's what he was capable of on the basketball court. I remember being so excited that I jumped over the ball players and folding chairs and ran out onto the floor to hug his tall frame.

We knew his potential and when he would come home complaining about this or that we would try to encourage him to just do his very best. We truly felt like he had a bright future in basketball. We attended all of his home games at Lincoln Trail College in Illinois which left David Sr. getting in bed at midnight and getting up at 5:30 a.m. to go to work. We often wondered if Davy truly appreciated our efforts.

When Davy was about 11, he did something that we thought was out of his character. When I learned of this incident, [3] I had this really sick feeling that he was involved. Upon questioning, he admitted to the wrong doing. We told him he would have to face and admit his wrong to the party involved. Later, as I was walking down the hallway, toward his

---

[3] This incident is in reference to a friend and me camping out in the backyard and breaking into the neighbor's house while they were gone on vacation. This was not the first time I had stolen but it was the first time I had gotten caught and it would not be the last time I stole or the last time I would get caught.

room, I found him kneeling on his knees in prayer. I thought at that moment that he was picking up on the principles that we were trying to teach him and all would be well.

This was only the beginning of the problems he would face during the course of his life. Our hearts would be crushed because of the breaking of God's commandments we had tried so hard to teach him through *"The Word of Wisdom."* I learned that this commandment alone brought the breaking of many more commandments that could destroy a person if they continued in it.

I heard someone say once that love and forgiveness is cut and dry, black and white. Either you love and forgive or you don't. It's as simple as that. We always chose to love and forgive, over and over and over again. And I guess through our imperfections, we have expected the same from our children.

When I hear of a child who has made a bad choice that has caused him or her to suffer, my heart goes out to the parent, who a good percentage of the time came from a similar background as David Sr. and I, and only wanted the best for their children.

I have lived my life through my faith in the scripture *"Train up a child in the way he should go; and when he is old, he will not depart from it"* (Proverbs 22:6 KJV). David Sr. and I both lived for that scripture. We never gave up hope that someday our first born would have a better life. That he would prosper and not look back, but move forward to a better life helping someone else who has struggled.

Love is an action that does what's best for the other person.[4] Parents' feelings of anger, because they didn't see the

---

[4] Paraphrase 1 Corinthians 13:4-8

23

warning signs, and then desperation to fix a problem that is out of their control is something I know all too well.]

My mother was right. I was out of control. I will share different accounts from my life of chaos sporadically throughout the book to bring to light some life applications at the end of each chapter that will bring hope to some hurting parents, or a wakeup call to some disobedient, rebellious children that are a lot like I once was.

# DEATH

At the time of the story I am about to share, I had been arrested at least eight times, served jail time for several of these arrests, been married and divorced twice, and married a third time to my current wife, Joy, for five years. And those are just a few examples of how insane my life was leading up to this cool fall day in 2004.

I usually wouldn't drink until after the work day was complete. That didn't mean that I never used other drugs or smoked pot throughout the day. That just meant I thought I could hide my drug abuse easier than if I openly drank beer on the job site.

It was about 5:30 p.m. and I had nearly finished a six pack, a couple of Xanax, and a few joints. I arrived at the temporary trailer Joy and I were living in while we built a new house. This place was a dump and the kitchen was not set up for cooking meals. I sent Joy to the country market to buy sandwiches for that night's dinner.

She hated to call me when trouble came because of how I would respond but on this evening she had no choice but to call. Her car had died going up a hill, and she called to tell me that the car was out of gas. I grunted and groaned and left with a gas can in the back of the truck and headed towards the car that was stalled only a few miles away.

I got in the car and it started right up so I cussed and acted like a complete idiot and let my wife know how much she was at fault. I sent her in my truck to Holt's, a local country market, to get dinner and I took off toward home in the car.

The ride back began on a steep incline that led me into the Guthrie bottoms, a winding valley filled with corn and soy bean fields. As I came out of the bottoms and proceeded to climb the first hill, the car began to spit and to sputter. The car died and came to a complete stop in the road. I was out of gas.

I always took pride in being able to get myself out of tight spots, but the truth is, I was not good at getting out of tight spots. I was good at lying, cheating, and deceiving myself by thinking I was good at getting out of tough places. I thought *"No problem, I will just let the car roll backwards building up enough speed to back into a driveway at the bottom of the hill and I will wait on Joy to come by."*

In the meantime, I was blocking one lane of traffic and there was not enough room to just leave the car since there was a steep hill over the shoulder and I had to do something because I had a beer between my legs, and I was not getting rid of my beer. As the car began to roll backwards, I began to cut the wheels into the driveway but realized that I did not have enough speed. I then found myself not blocking one lane of traffic but two. As I sat horizontally across the roadway I decided, *"okay, now I may want to get rid of the beer."* Left with no choice except to try and push the vehicle out of the road, I began rocking the vehicle back and forth trying to get it up over the hump in the driveway and out of the road.

As I think about myself rocking the car back and forth, I am reminded today of how this is symbolic with living for God and being pulled back into the world. It was at this current place in life that God was trying to turn me around. This could have been that experience that brought awakening, but it became another unexplainable scenario that I blew off and God brought back to my remembrance later.

25

As I rocked the car back and forth, it was almost ready to get over the hump, but the car broke free from my control and began to move forward. When I saw that the car was moving forward at an unstoppable pace, I tried in a last ditch effort to stick my foot into the moving vehicle to press the brake. As I lunged for the brake pedal, my foot got stuck under it, and I found myself hooked and on my back in a bad situation.

I recall the picture of me trying to press the brake on the moving car as great symbolism for my life. In my life, I was hooked on drugs and alcohol, and my life was out of control. I tried to press the brake on this lifestyle many times, but it kept on dragging me into dangerous places much like the moving car was dragging me in this story.

As the car led me down the treacherous hillside, bouncing me off of God's green earth and asphalt, I could not help but see what was coming towards me. It was a barbed wire fence and all I could think was that this is going to hurt. As the car tore through the fence and ripped through the barbed wire, all I could do was cover my face. Somehow, I was freed from the vehicle at that moment. Still on my back, I leaned up on my elbows and witnessed something I had only ever seen on television.

The car continued to pick up speed and it was out of control. I watched the car ramp off a cliff in the middle of the hill. The scene reminded me of Bo and Luke Duke from the television show *"Dukes of Hazard."* The sound of the crash and the glass breaking quickly turned into reality, though.

I sat there for a few seconds that seemed like an eternity, and I felt something telling me that my life was no different than what I had just witnessed. My life was out of control. I snapped into survival mode and gathered myself quickly because surely no one had witnessed this event, and I needed to exit the area quickly or I might get arrested for driving under the influence.

I looked up and it appeared no one was around until I looked off into the distance and on the ridge of a far-off hill were three horses with three riders. Seriously, I thought, three witnesses watching the whole thing from horseback. One of the riders was in full pursuit to come and check on me to see if I was all right. I brushed myself off and waved him off from a distance in a way that let him know I was fine.

As I turned toward the road there was a car sitting there and a female driver whose eyes were about to pop out of her head. She too had seen the whole thing and asked me if she could do anything to help me out and I quickly said, *"Yes, you can give me a ride out of here."*

Once again my life was spared, yet I was still running from God and back to a world of misery. As soon as I got home, I opened a beer, and when Joy returned I began yelling at her. I was a stupid idiot projecting blame towards her as if it was her fault I almost died.

This near death experience put some temporary fear into me, but at the time I had so much baggage that I did not have a clue where to begin shedding my addictions. I was so lost and under so much persuasion that it was only going to get worse before it would get better.

At this point in life I was a ticking time bomb and a walking dead man. Things did get worse over the next year because I began using heroin. I've done a lot of drugs over my lifetime and been addicted to all of them, but nothing was worse than this drug. I couldn't function without it. I was sick with it, and I was sick without it. There was no way I could escape the clutches of this drug without going through a season of being "dope sick" but I also knew I had to stop.

My life was going nowhere fast, and if something didn't change quickly I was a dead man. I remember crying out to God to get me off this stuff. I didn't want Him to be Lord but I wanted to be healed from this drug, so I began to seek Him for help. His help was on the way, but since He had been in pursuit of me for about eight years, things were going to get ugly while He was at work behind the scenes.

In the early summer of 2005, a couple of dope friends and I headed up to Indianapolis for a heroin pick-up. The dealer on this night was a different supplier than who we usually used. His product was always high quality but light on the scales. We made our pick-up and headed out of Indianapolis stopping at a convenient store so one of the guys could get high in the bathroom. We all were addicted and had it bad; however, this guy had it the worst. I broke him off a little piece of this stuff but really couldn't tell how much it was or how good it was. The problem with heroin is that it can be dangerously high in quality or it could be junk.

We waited for him to come out of the bathroom and finally, I told my other friend he would have to go in and check on him to see if he was all right. When he returned, he said that the door was locked and no one answered when he knocked. I told him he would have to take his driver's license and pick the lock to see if our friend was all right. He went in and came back telling me that our friend was out cold, face down on the floor, a syringe beside him, and his belt off just like what you would see in the movies. Except this was really happening.

We discussed briefly what we should do and weighed our options quickly. I had always prided myself as being a tough guy who would never leave a brother behind or snitch on a friend. We had a couple of choices and not much time to make a decision. I could take the heroin that was in my pocket and place it into the trash can and go help my friend, or I could keep my heroin and leave my friend to die. I chose to leave my friend to die and we drove off and headed back to Bloomington.

That decision was insane, and of course I was high, but that's no excuse because I knew full well what I was doing. We returned to a safe house and made contact with his girlfriend. She came to where we were and we told her the news. She began making phone calls to Indianapolis hospitals as she sat and got high with us. We found out after about six hours around 4:00 a.m. that he was found in the bathroom and an ambulance was sent to revive him. We made arrangements to pick him up at the hospital, divided up the dope and went on with our everyday lives.

After the cloud cleared the next evening, I thought hard about the line that I had crossed, and I could not believe that I had chosen a drug over another person's life. I really did like this guy which proved to me in a major way that I was a mess and my life was seriously out of control.

That same evening, the phone rang and I knew it was my friend. I was ashamed and hesitant to even answer. Upon answering, I began to ask him if he could forgive me for what I had done and that I really could not believe that I had left him there to die.

And this is what my friend said to me, "It's cool bro, I would have done the same thing to you. Do you need any dope?"

Those words went through me and shook me at the very core of my being. Something changed in me at that moment and I made the decision that I was done with this destructive addiction. My response to him was *"No, I am done."*

*High on heroin, mushrooms, beer, and weed
during the summer of 2005*

# LIFE

It wasn't the car going over the cliff or the fact that I had no value of life that finally led me to complete surrender to Christ, but these were pivotal defining moments in my life that God used to bring me to a place where I would have to rely on someone besides myself.

I stopped using heroin at that moment and over the next few weeks the withdrawals were crazy bad. My wife had to change the sheets every night and put up with my out of control, full-body jerks. The days were hard and the nights were long. I still had resources and investments in other drugs and money that would hinder me from complete surrender to Christ. Even though I beat the heroin addiction, I was still doing things my way which continued to lead me down the path of destruction.

I had a close friend who was also a partner in the drug culture who had been arrested in 2003 for federal cultivation of marijuana drug offense. I thought it wise to shift my interest into another market since I was under the watchful eye of law enforcement. My partner gave me permission to continue making business transactions from his assets while he was in federal prison. I attempted to make money in the housing market but my addiction and unstable thinking caused our investments to become more than I could keep up with.

In a last ditch effort to save everything, I invested in a hydroponic and organics shop called Organics Plus located in Bloomington, Indiana.

My idea for the shop was to make the equipment available to people who chose to enter into illegal activity. Indoor gardening was something I had experience with and enjoyed, but that hobby was now limited by obstacles that God allowed in my life. I was so stiff-necked, rebellious and always leaned on my own understanding in everything I did. He was serious about removing me from this lifestyle all together.

*Hydroponic grown basil at Organics Plus in 2005*

From 2003 through 2005 I successfully wasted away close to $400,000. Some of that money was in property, but most of it was simply gone. Everything had been maxed out so there was no equity in any of the properties. My partner's release was just around the corner. I was desperately hoping to have dealt with all this debt before his release. Since that didn't happen, I quickly grew concerned about the wrath of my partner once he found out about my failures.

At this point, I sat behind the counter of *"Organics Plus"* and just cried. I was out of strength and out of money. I had nothing left but God. My wife was sick of the insanity and had no confidence left in me. She was disgusted by me. I had become so bad that the love she once had was no longer available.

Finally, I asked God to take over my life on November 1, 2005. I was sick and tired of being sick and tired, and it was time to surrender everything to His sovereign control. I know that he met with me that day and gave me a new life through Jesus Christ. The road was going to be difficult and hard, but I found new life in Christ. What Satan meant for evil the Lord meant for good

Since then I have learned how to die to myself and come alive for God which means I lay down my life. I was not raised in a broken home or a home of horrible parents. The sin nature is born into every human creature on this planet. Unless we are willing to lay down our life and die like Jesus explains in John 12:24-26, we cannot come to life in Christ:

> *[Very truly I tell you, unless a kernel of wheat falls to the ground and dies, it remains only a single seed. But if it dies, it produces many seeds. Anyone who loves their life will lose it, while anyone who hates their life in this world will keep it for eternal life. Whoever serves me must follow me; and where I am, my servant also will be. My Father will honor the one who serves me.]*

Most of us struggle with surrender, laying down our life, and dying to our self. Becoming obedient and submissive to His commands is not religious control but freedom. Jesus rebuked the religious and self-righteous but also confronted the condemned sinner. None of us want to be confronted or rebuked, but it is this mindset that leads many people to false conversions. Sin must be confronted in our life and dealt with through complete surrender to the Lordship of Jesus Christ. It is then that we will receive resurrection power and a new life.

Many of us want this resurrection power because it sounds so good "I want to know Christ—yes, to know the power of his resurrection and participation in his sufferings, becoming like him in his death," (Philippians 2:10 NIV).

The truth of the gospel is that we cannot participate in the power of the resurrection unless we have fallen to the ground and died to our own wants and desires. This message is what causes most of us to stumble. Will you suffer for Him and die to any desires that are not His for your life?

God is not a token to a happy and comfortable life but a God that sent His own Son to suffer and die for the sins of the world. Oh, we want resurrection power but are we willing to suffer for Him and die to ourselves to really live? If so, that means living for His glory, His kingdom, His mission, His purpose.

I am free because I have been set free by the life of Christ working in and through me. The Bible says, "Do your best to present yourself to God as one approved, a worker who has no need to be ashamed, rightly handling the word of truth. (2 Timothy 2:15 ESV).

I am forgiven and walking in truth and grace. I am persecuted, insulted, falsely accused for His name's sake on a regular basis. I am not ashamed because it is not for me I live, but for Him I died. The Bible says that just like the prophets who came before Him, I will be mistreated, but when these persecutions and insults come I am more than free, I am blessed.[5]

Submission is not a frequently accepted behavior in our culture. But rebellion is a behavior that every individual can relate to on a personal level. In the next chapter I will share how Jesus taught me to say no to rebellion and yes to submission.

---

[5] Paraphrase of Matthew 5:11-12 "Blessed are you when people insult you, persecute you and falsely say all kinds of evil against you because of me. Rejoice and be glad, because great is your reward in heaven, for in the same way they persecuted the prophets who were before you" NIV

# -2-

# From Rebellion to Submission

*Submit to God's sovereignty
and life will go well with you.*

*Because you have raged against me and your complacency
has come to my ears, I will put my hook in your nose and
my bit in your mouth, and I will turn you back on the way by
which you came.*

Isaiah 37:29 ESV

One of the greatest needs in our culture today is a willingness to submit to authority. Mark Driscoll, a controversial emerging church leader, and Pastor has stated, *"Our culture considers nearly all rebellion against any authority inherently noble. We forget that the first rebellion was started by Satan."[6]* Rebellion is one of the reasons this country is in big trouble.

Our culture today considers rebellion good. We put rebellion on a pedestal in hopes that the more attention we bring to ourselves, the more our Godless society will notice us. In the news and entertainment industry, if it doesn't bleed, it doesn't lead. Watching and participating in sinful activities is amusing to a lot of us. We enjoy watching the good fall and the rebellious rewarded.

---

[6] Mark Driscoll, facebook post

35

This form of entertainment and thinking is wrong. It is not from the God of the Bible but from the god of this world. There are too few courageous people who are willing to stand against this attitude of rebellion because in order to do so, we must first identify our own rebellion. Rebellion can be discovered in our hearts by looking deep into our attitude towards submission to God's sovereign control over our life.

Our culture today is insisting that Jesus was a rebel. This cultural view that Jesus was a rebel says that Christianity is in desperate need of Spirit-led rebels to rise up against the authority of the traditional church. This approach is an unashamed lack of respect and honor and a direct result of a rebellious people that is no longer submitting to the authority of God. Jesus was not a rebel; we are the rebels. He is the authority, and life will go well for us when we submit to His authority.

Rebellion has such a negative connotation that many in our culture do not consider themselves rebellious; however, when we analyze rebellion through God's eyes, all of us can see rebellion in some way in ourselves even if we don't follow a journey where rebellion is very obvious.

Recognizing rebellion and how to stop it is a part of everyone's journey to discipleship. The solution to rebellion is not to go against governing authorities or the church but to submit to the sovereignty of a just God. I hope you will read this book in a way that you can discover your own discipleship journey and that requires you to find new insight and thought to topics that you have already heard before, like submission and rebellion.

Here are a few responses of a rebel that demonstrate an absent or weak relationship with God where He and His Word are not the deciding factor. *"Who's in charge...Who do they think they are... Don't you tell me...and I know (this is the worst one for me to hear)."*

God is in charge and his authority guides us. Trying to know everything is idolatry.

The solution to rebellion in our country is not to create more laws but to submit to the laws we already have. The reason we continue to create more laws is because as a whole we are rebellious towards authority. We blame drugs, guns, and pornography as the big issues, but in God's eyes unforgiveness, bitterness, idolatry, adultery, factions, divisions, sorcery, and partying are real rebellion. So, it seems sin is the real problem because when our hearts are not turned towards God, we are rebellious.

God's solution is for us to love others more then we love ourselves. If we love anything more than we love God, then we are rebelling against God's plan for our life. All of the laws in our society could be summed up by two laws of God *"And you shall Love the Lord your God with all your heart ... soul...mind, and strength. The second ...Love your neighbor as yourself... "* (Mark 12:30-31ESV).

So the question is who do you love? Most of us are filled with self-love first and that explains why we do what we do. My rebellion was always fueled by self-love. I did not love God or my neighbor but lusted after the good God could provide or the goods my neighbors had. This explains why I did the things I did.

## REBELLION

Rebellion against authority was my biggest problem in life. I could not submit or come under any God-ordained authority; therefore, I could not live in relationship with God because I was rebellious to His Word.

When I was a child, I felt like everything had to make sense to me and I demanded an explanation if something did not make sense. Why do we have to go here? Why do we have to do this? And I always had a good comeback for why I disagreed. This attitude was ridiculous and rebellious.

Before I met Christ, I was pathetic and disgusting and my life was full of self-love and idolatry. All that consumed me was what I wanted, when I wanted it, and what I could do to get it. That was how I approached life until my rebellion reached God's ears and my idolatry was all he could take. It was Christ that turned my life around; He transformed me and showed me grace that I did not deserve and for that I am glad.

There were many times in my life when I struggled with authority and submission. I hope by sharing a few examples of my struggles, others will be led to the same freedom I found through submission to God's authority and discover free will to make the right choices.

My inability to come under authority was a direct result of a disobedient, rebellious spirit. Many times I thought I was doing the right things, but my heart was still far from submission to God's purpose.

Prior to junior high school, I grew up in a church that practiced corporate fasting throughout the whole denomination. On the first Sunday of every month most families fasted and were taught that the food they didn't consume should be given to the poor. I was such a rebellious son that after communion was passed I would slip out of the church service into the kitchen and scarf down the leftover communion bread. My unwillingness to submit to authority was driving me to think only of my own flesh, regardless of whether I understood what I was doing or not.

In junior high I gave in to the pressure of wanting to be cool and became willing to do anything to fit in. I was deceived into believing that I needed to do bad things to get attention and be accepted. It was at this age that I really began to become defiant to my parents. I was caught several times using tobacco, lying, and stealing. These were behaviors that my parents were not willing to budge on disciplining me, but even still, I was not willing to change these youthful lusts. In other words, my unwillingness to come under their authority fueled my rebellion out of control.

I had a lot of friends whose parents would allow them to use tobacco, watch immoral TV, come home after curfew, and participate in other rebellious acts. I wanted to exchange my parents for their parents just so I could be free to do what I wanted. At that time in my life I hated my parents, and I was embarrassed by the Mormon religion and their god. I wanted what every other kid had, and I wanted to do everything the other kids were allowed to do.

Music was a major contributor to my rebellious spirit. Even as strict as my parents were, they really didn't interfere with my selection in music. They did not understand that allowing me to listen to rock music would be one of the instruments that I would use to invite evil and wicked spirits into my life.

Music during the 80's was a time of revolution. The rebellious chant was sung in a song by Twisted Sister that went like this, *"We're not going to take it anymore,"* and I got on board with that junk, and I shook my fist at my parents and at God, and literally sold my soul to the Devil to live in sin.

I have learned that the Holy Spirit and demonic spirits are alike in one way; they both require an invitation. You invite good or you invite evil into your life by the decisions you make. I chose to invite evil into my life through worldly music, one of the gateways that Satan uses to deceive so many.

Today, I find myself inside my home and ministry rejecting this rebellious music and will not allow my children or students to listen to anything except Christian music inside the home, ministry, or our vehicles. My parents wish they would have done some things differently in raising me, but even if they had, it wouldn't have mattered. They were not the ones with the problem. I was. I had no respect or honor towards my parents or the authority they had over my life.

I was driving my parents crazy and they realized that spiritual counsel was not working because I was not willing to receive it. I remember the day they sought counsel from outside the Church. My mom picked me up from school to take me to a therapy session. Upon arriving at the center I noticed the sign on the building "Mental Health Center." I was furious, so these sessions were nothing but a game of cat and mouse between the therapist and me. I tried to convince the therapist that all of our family's problems were due to my parents' Mormon church and their god. I was so prideful and full of myself that this brought major embarrassment when I had to return to school with physician notes that said "Mental Health Center" in big bold letters. After being humiliated on several occasions as a result of my own actions, I just started losing the excuse notes.

I hated authority so much that I ran away on several occasions. This led to getting arrested and being placed on probation for a few years when I was a teenager. Every time I ran away and had to come back, I hated authority even more. I would always run away to a friend's house where I was allowed to continue my rebellious behavior.

Now that I reflect back, these parents that would allow me to come and stay until I was forced to return had no true love for me and no relationship with God. It was easy for me to convince them that my parents were just religious nuts.

My rebellion and pride turned me into a know-it-all who didn't listen to anyone. My actions were the evidence of what I refer to as full-blown rebellion. When I think of rebellion, I look at it with two definitions, inward and outward rebellion.

My rebellion started inward when my heart began to stray from authority. I still did all the things that I was asked to do, but on the inside I was not submissive. I still went to school even though I couldn't stand school. I still went to church but hated every minute I was there. I cussed around my friends, but I would never cuss around my mom and dad or any authority figure.

Outward rebellion follows inward rebellion. For instance, since I resented going to school, I began to openly speak about how much I hated school. In the same way, I hated going to church and began to show that hatred by challenging my parent's beliefs and demanding the right to live differently. Furthermore, I no longer filtered my perverse language. I cussed when I wanted, where I wanted, and at whom I wanted. These examples were evidence of a heart that despised authority.

Perhaps the most impactful decision I made during my rebellious outburst was my decision to quit church my freshman year. I recall the morning very well and I remember planning it out the night before. I was simply just not going to go. As usual my mother attempted to wake me up around 8:00a.m. because we had to leave by 9:00a.m. I laid there for as long as I could without saying a word, pretending I was unable to be stirred. She became furious that I was not getting up. I didn't care, though. I told her that I was not going and that was my final decision. I told her that she could beat me, ground me, and send me off to boy school, but I was done. I quit.

My Dad always went to church early for leadership meetings, so he was already gone. My mom called him and demanded he come and get me out of bed. Before my father arrived, I made up my mind that I was not going to move. He threatened me and I rebelled against his authority as I denounced their church and their god. I wanted nothing to do with this part or any other part of their life. As I reflect back on this moment, I am disgusted at my rebellion and I have no one to blame but myself. I dug my cleats into a new phase of rebellion that morning.

I got what I asked for and my life bore the fruit of rebellion. I was forced through the law and the courts to remain at home until I turned eighteen. At eighteen I walked out from under the protection of my parents and into a world that I so desired. This led to deeper and more deceptive rebellion as God's Word describes *"...they did not wait for His counsel, but lusted exceedingly in the wilderness, and tested God in the desert. And he gave them their request, But sent leanness into their soul"* (Psalm 106:13-15 NIV). My desire was to be lawless and to be as good as possible at being bad, without getting caught.

From the age of 18 to the age of 25, I was able to avoid being charged with any illegal activity so this led to an attitude of thinking I was invincible. It wasn't until my second marriage to Brandy that I was caught in my illegal affairs.

On January 19, 1995, the cops burst into Brandy's and my house for a big marijuana bust. We knew there was a good chance we were going to be raided so we spent that morning cleaning house. We had no loose pot or any white inside the house. In our eyes there was no visible evidence of being the home of drug dealers. We wiped down every mirror, tabletop, and tool that might have been used in the distribution of drugs. The one thing that I rebelled against disposing was the grow operation that was in the basement.

I remember making this statement to Brandy, *"If they come rolling in on us I will go down for something I believe in."* That statement shows how out of control my thinking was. Growing pot is against the law, but since I felt like it was acceptable, my opinion was above the law and this showed how I wanted to be king of my life.

They arrested my wife with me, and our four-month-old daughter was sent to our daycare provider. We were able to bond out as fast as we were booked in. This only puffed me up more and caused me to think I was somebody. Pride always comes before a fall but not even this experience was big enough to stop my rebellious heart.

After the bust, our drug abuse moved into its absolute most devastating phase. We began manufacturing and cooking a new drug called *"CAT"* and we moved into a weekly motel where we began making a batch of dope at least once a week. I was cooking dope inside a motel room, using needles to get high, and packing a 9mm in my back with my daughter in the same room. If people do not see how this sick and twisted behavior was born out of rebellion and wickedness from Satan's invitations, then I pray God opens their eyes. This lifestyle is straight up sickening.

We were evicted from the motel and Brandy left me for another guy. At this time in life I was beginning to see how lost I had become. I was weaker than I had ever been, yet I was still too proud to confess that I was a loser who needed help!

I was going through some serious spiritual warfare without even realizing it. I didn't understand what was happening, but it was scaring me to death. The drugs I allowed to consume my life brought with them so many demonic spirits that they caused me to lose my mind. The devil was really playing tricks on me so much so that I was unsure of reality and full of fear and paranoia. I look back now and understand that Satan was out to destroy me because he wanted me dead.

My rebellion reached a plateau in1996 as I entered a cold and empty bedroom that had become my place of safety. I locked the door behind me and quickly closed the blinds. I was ashamed of what I had become. I was hopelessly living a life of insanity and I couldn't find safety anywhere because I couldn't control my desire to get high. Even though I opened the door to this addiction, I never believed I would wind up being this kind of guy who was this sick, scared, and utterly lost.

As I reached into my pocket for a syringe and a spoon I was thirsting for something more than the evil of that needle. With disgust, I injected poison into my veins. In a rush, I was in the

43

presence of demonic forces and I suddenly hated what I was fighting so hard to obtain. I knew at that moment someone or something was out to destroy me. I could feel its presence consuming me so much that I couldn't hide. No matter where I was, it found me and watched my every move.

I thought to myself, *"What does it want with me and why is it tormenting me? Where can I go? Who can I trust? Someone please HELP ME!"* I didn't know who was controlling my mind or whether to trust the voices inside me. I got out a pen and paper to write down my thoughts and clear my head, but as I was writing, the same words appeared over and over on every page, *"HELP ME, HELP ME, HELP ME..."*

I still wasn't convinced God was real, but I continued to question why he would allow me to survive so many close calls with death just for me to be in this place, writing over and over, *"HELP ME."* How did my life come to a place where I was so empty, void, and lost that I found myself crying out to a piece of paper or anyone who could hear my cry for help? I desperately needed help.

I believe God heard my cry through all this insanity. I knew nothing about God because I had not invited the Holy Spirit into my heart. Instead, I invited and welcomed evil into my heart through my years of rebellion, and it scared me to death. I was running, but God came to my rescue. It didn't happen the way I wanted but the Lord is very merciful and longsuffering. In my cry for help, He was preparing to take me to a place where I would be safe and have the opportunity to hear the good news of the gospel of Jesus Christ. God works in mysterious ways, because the place He was preparing me for was jail.

Within a few months after I cried out for help, I found myself homeless and driving around looking for a place to hide so I could get high. I drove down to the White River boat dock right off of Highway 37. I thought I could hang out there until morning. I wanted to get wasted so I filled up two syringes of dope. I stuck one syringe in a vein in my leg and injected the other one into my arm which was ridiculous. I should have been dead and I believe I was very close to crossing over in that moment. This was the first time since I cried out for help that I felt this close to death and immediately I began to wig out, which is the drug culture's slang for freak out. The details of the illusions I had that night are not worth repeating. It was only the cop cars approaching that brought me back to reality.

They approached me and informed me that they were going to search the vehicle. Upon searching the vehicle, they found several empty syringes, two switch blade knives, a box of battery acid, and some tubing. Outside the vehicle they found a syringe with a clear liquid inside. There was no way for me to get out of this situation. I was sent to jail and served nine months on a probation violation before I was able to bond out on the charge of possession of methamphetamine. Jail is ultimately where my rebellion took me.

Rebellion will take those that don't turn towards God to bondage or the grave. The beautiful thing is that I asked for help that night in the bedroom and that is exactly what I got. Jail was the help that I needed at that time in my life because it was during that period that I would have the gospel of Jesus Christ presented to me in a place where I could not run.

## SUBMISSION

In 2009, I began to write the stories about my life. I was learning to submit to God and His plans for my life, I thought I was ready to share my story but as I read over my notes in 2014, I could see that in 2009 I was not ready to share it in a way that would bring Christ glory. The fact that I was still blaming the discipline of my parents, coaches, and teachers for my rebellion showed that I was not actually free yet. How could I possibly write a book on being free while continuing to make excuses and offer unbalanced Biblical comebacks for why I disagreed with how my parents' decided to raise me and how coaches, and teachers chose to discipline me.

I have learned that my way of living, thinking, and making decisions do not bring glory to God. My plans and purposes always fall short of God's ultimate and eternal desire for my life. I must die to myself and become willing to live for God first and others second. To do this I must believe that God is who He says He is and that I am not the authority over my own life. In rebellion, I ruled my own life, but now, I surrender and submit to an all-knowing, authoritative God.

This submission begins with faith in Jesus being the *"the Christ, the Son of the living God"* (Matthew 16: 16 ESV) and this confession leads to proper disciplines and exercises of *"a spiritual journey."* It is not by our works we are saved, but because we are saved and surrendered to Christ, we go to work and are able to submit to his divine, sovereign plan for our lives. A true conversion and transformed life will always lead to willing submission and obedience to a sovereign God.

Our ability to submit is directly related to our understanding of God's sovereignty. Unless God is totally sovereign in our heart, we will not know how to make sense of submission. Sovereignty means that God is independent of all, the supreme ruler of all, and has the capacity to control His will in all things. Understanding God's sovereignty is essential to submission.

Knowing God is sovereign means I don't have to rely on believers to keep me accountable because I understand God is viewing my entire life, but my understanding of who God is develops a desire to be surrounded by believers that will hold me accountable to my confession. God wants us to hold each other accountable, but if we live to please our accountability groups rather than God, we will fail in our attempt to please man above God. It's God alone that keeps me accountable to live a holy life and I place myself under His protection by submitting to His Word, His purpose, and His people.

This is the way I choose to live my life *"And no creature is hidden from his sight, but all are naked and exposed to the eyes of him to whom we must give account"* (Hebrews 4:13 ESV). I remind myself often that God is sovereign and I am not. I feel liberated knowing that if I do not confess all of my sin, God will reveal my sin to me. Remember, whatever sin I expose through confession and being real with God, He will cover with His amazing grace. On the other hand, whatever I try to hide from God, He will reveal in due time.

There is always a choice to be free and live in God's sovereign will. God is absolutely sovereign and we have a free will to choose a life of blessing or cursing. God's sovereignty and our free will working together is complex to us because it's hard to understand how we can have a free will if God's sovereign plan will take place regardless of what we choose. But that is what makes God infinite and us finite. God designed such complexity between His sovereignty and our free will in order to lead us to a deeper understanding of His unfailing love.

We must learn to understand that God does not love according to our definition of love. God's ways are not our ways, and God's love is not a pampering love. God's love is a perfecting love. God does not wake up every day to see how he can put a bigger smile on our face. Rather, God disciplines and chastens while still being gentle, compassionate, merciful, and long suffering. In His sovereignty, he allows good and painful things to happen. We need to recognize that He is still in control, even in painful conditions. God desires that these situations grow us closer to Him. But we must come to Him even when it is painful or we will only grow further from Him.

God doesn't have to give us a reason for putting difficult situations in our lives. He just asks that we accept what comes our way because He has allowed it. This is His will and when we do the will of God, there is no reason to dispute his plans for our life.

We must look to scripture to understand how God establishes his delegated authority in our life. We are instructed to *"Obey your leaders and submit to them, for they are keeping watch over your souls, as those who will have to give an account. Let them do this with joy and not with groaning, for that would be of no advantage to you"* (Hebrews 13:17 ESV). The only way for me to come out of rebellion was to learn how to submit first to God and then also to those he has given authority to in my life, and only then was I able to be free at last.

We are taught that it is God who establishes authority and if we want life to go well for us then we must submit to those he has given authority to in our life. Those that submit and do no wrong have no fear of those in authority, *"For rulers are not a terror to good conduct, but to bad. Would you have no fear of the one who is in authority? Then do what is good, and you will receive his approval,"* (Romans 13:3 ESV). If you want to be free from the wrath that rebellion brings, then you must **submit to God's sovereignty and life will go well with you.**

Every soul will answer to an all-knowing sovereign God. Every man and woman will be left with no excuse for not submitting to the authority of God. The Bible teaches *"so that at the name of Jesus every knee should bow, in heaven and on earth and under the earth, and every tongue confess that Jesus Christ is Lord, to the glory of God the Father."* (Philippians 2:10-11ESV). People will either bow now or they will bow at the judgment seat of Christ.

This chapter only touched the surface of the freedom that can be found when one moves from rebellion to submission. But what I hope changed in you is what changed in me and that was realizing how God is great and I am not. How God is sovereign and I am not. How God is in control and I am not. How God is at work and I am His workman that need not be ashamed.

God demonstrates how powerful He is through transforming and changing lives daily. I am only one of countless others that he has transformed. God does not need us to accomplish His will, but we need Him.

At this point in my disciple's journey, I was still a rebellious criminal sentenced to nine months in county jail. I so desperately needed God, and in his power and perfect timing, he transformed a criminal like me to his faithful servant.

# -3-

# From Criminal to Christian

## *Stop being a scatterer and become a gatherer*

*"Whoever is not with me is against me, and whoever does not gather with me scatters"*

Matthew 12:30 ESV

There comes a time in every person's life when they must make a choice to be a scatterer, leading people away from Christ, or a gatherer, leading people to Christ.

This metaphorical use of the terms *"scatterer"* and *"gatherer"* is used in a parable in Matthew 12: 22-32 about a religious group accusing Jesus of being a lawbreaker and performing miracles through an evil spirit. Jesus's response to the accusations is a simple statement but an eternal message for Christians, *"Whoever is not with me is against me, and whoever does not gather with me scatters"* (Matthew 12:30 ESV).

Jesus' words here confront those that reject the Holy Spirit and separates people into two separate groups, those that scatter and those that gather. According to Jesus, those that scatter are in danger of committing the only unforgivable sin which is blasphemy of the Holy Ghost. Those that gather are safe and secure walking in the spirit. So there are two forces at work in the world, gathering and scattering. Whoever does one contradicts the other.

When we understand these two forces at work, we realize being a Christian is more than just making the decision to join God's team. Every day we must choose to be gatherers for Christ because with everything we say and everything we do, we are either helping gather people together under His wings or we are scattering people to the furthest reaches away from the church and any desire to be a part of His Kingdom.

Being a gatherer is, at times, easier said than done, but we must constantly strive to be gatherers so we don't lose our witness by speaking words or engaging in behaviors that will damage our testimony by not glorifying God. If what we say and what we do bring no glory to God, then we are scattering people away from God. As a result, we cause confusion and conflict in God's church and His kingdom.

So I ask you as I've asked myself, what position do you take? Do you speak with grace, thankfulness, and love to bring glory to God and gather people to His covenant of love, and create in them a desire to seek God?

Or, do you spend so much time complaining, back biting, gossiping, or being bitter that you focus more time thinking about how so and so hurt you or isn't treating you the way they should? If you relate more to the second scenario, then my friend you too, as I am sometimes, are a scatterer. This is not the title that I want and I hope you agree with me too.

Maybe you don't feel you are scattering to that extreme, but what are you doing to further God's kingdom? If you are doing nothing, you are just as guilty of scattering because remember the first half of the verse, *"Whoever is not with Me is against Me..."* Therefore, if we are not doing anything bad, but at the same time not doing anything to bring Him glory, we are against Him and causing destruction.

Robbing God of His purpose and glory by scattering souls away from Him is how we are all criminals. When we truly transform from criminal to Christian, we stop robbing God, scattering, and start blessing God, gathering, by doing our Christian duty rather than just talking about it.

Being a Christian is so much more than saying, *"I am a Christian."* Once we proclaim Christ, we live with purpose each day, choosing our words and actions carefully so that we glorify God and help gather the sheep so the Shepherd can nurture their wounds, heal their scars, and teach them to love Him more than life itself.

## "CRIMINAL"

It was 1997, and I was a common criminal who would live the next nine months of my life hearing new phrases like *"What kind of bird don't fly? A jail bird!!!"* Or a prisoner responding to the judge when he couldn't pay his fines, *"You can't squeeze blood out of a rock"* and the judge's response back, *"I can put the rock in jail."*

Jail is the final resting place for dead men that are still breathing. These men have not yet chosen to obey the authority of the law. Jail is also the worst educational facility on the planet to learn how to be a Christian; however, jail can be the end of an old life or the start of a new life depending on whether or not the prisoner will continue in rebellion. As for me, I didn't make the right decision right away when I arrived at jail, but eventually I figured out that doing time in jail was not what I wanted to do for the rest of my life, so I knew I had to change.

I believe my criminal acts and my scattering developed in the early years of elementary. I became resourceful in supporting my addiction to chewing tobacco that began in third grade. I always found ways to hide my habit from my parents and searched continuously for ways to come up with money to support my addiction. I would steal through any opportunity that presented itself.

I stole from my father's wallet, my mom's purse, kids at school, and I used my lunch money for the week to buy chew. My stealing escalated to taking the payment envelopes out of newspaper mailboxes at the beginning of every month.

Eventually, I got caught, but getting caught stealing only inspired me to plan out my next thieving scheme and to do it better.

My friend and I were camping out in the backyard when I was 12 years old and we were out of chewing tobacco and knew the neighbor was a user and on vacation. We broke into his house and my friend laid on the ground and protected me with a BB gun as I climbed in through the window. We did not find any chew, cigarettes, or alcohol, but we did find a coin collection that we used the next morning to purchase some chew and candy at the local country store.

Later on during my freshman year of high school, I had a friend who owned every rock tape ever produced. When I asked him how he could afford all those tapes, he told me that he doesn't buy them; he steals them. My mom dropped us off at the mall one night to hang out, and he showed me how he was able to steal so easily.

At the first store we went to everything went as planned, but our plan did not go so well in the second store. We were caught, so my first night of shoplifting ended with both of us at the police station for my first run-in directly with the police.

Even though I had my first run-in with the police, I still continued looking for ways to continue my criminal behavior. As a newly licensed driver, I was now on the hunt for beer trucks, farmer's gas pumps, and girlfriends that would support my sexual desires. Eventually, I graduated to distributing large quantities of drugs and left those petty criminal acts to beginners.

In 1997, when I found myself being transported to jail from the White River arrest without any money, hopeless, and close to the end of myself, I was tempted to cross the line of telling on someone else to free myself. I was at a place in my life where I knew that I was really sick and that I needed help more than ever. The problem with this was that I was the one they wanted off the streets more than any other dealer.

I was nervous as I was on my way to jail. I was booked in and charged with manufacturing methamphetamine, possession of methamphetamine, reckless paraphernalia, and possession of switch blade knives. I was placed in detox for at least three days and up to five days; I'm not sure. I crashed so hard that I lost track of time. Finally, they came to move me to population and I ended up in E-Block which was only a four man block. I spent about 60 days in this block where eventually I had a stunning encounter with God.

The first 45 days I had to learn how to adapt to this new lifestyle. I had a girlfriend on the streets, and a wife that was not interested in reconciliation. The first decision that I made after watching and listening to other inmates struggle with women and their unfaithfulness was to purge myself early and get rid of my girlfriend, Amber, quickly. At our first visit I explained to Amber that I cared for her; however, for my health and her future it would be best for her to move on with life.

After two or three weeks a guy by the name of Bobby Garrison came in and became my roommate.[7] He had some daring drug connections on the outside and we had a want on the inside. Bobby wasn't a rookie to the system so this wasn't his first time in jail.

Bobby quickly began to teach me how to embezzle drugs into the jail. He removed a piece of metal from the mop ring and we both whittled a hole through the mortar of our window in our cell block just big enough to get a straw through. He began making calls to the outside and had drugs sent in through the hole. They would pack a straw full of Meth, cocaine, or pills and someone would walk by the

---

[7] Bobby Garrison died in late 2008 or early 2009 of a drug overdose

jail and slip it through the hole. We got really brave one night and had a syringe passed into the jail. Here I was locked up and still finding ways to shoot up dope. Word got out among the inmates and we were sure the jail officers would find out that we had a hole in the wall, so we went to the bunk next door, drilled a new hole, and then turned our hole in as if it had always been there.

As I continued this criminal behavior in jail, I began to grow tired of such a lifestyle. I started to read a little bit of the Bible but I did not understand what I was reading. I began to pray one night after attending my first jail service in which I thought the man preaching was talking right at me.

My attitude towards him made me think, "Who does this man think he is?" but I began to pray, "God, if you are really out there and you want me to read this book then you are going to have to help me understand what it says. As a matter of fact, you are going to have to give it to me in a comic book form."

I was serious, and I would soon realize that God was going to get serious with me. I never told anybody what I prayed. As a matter of fact, I was too cool to tell anyone I had even prayed. Within just a few days I was still trying to read and understand the Bible, but I was really confused, discouraged, and about to give up.

Then, through the bean hole (the slot they pass in the food trays) came flying a little story book version of the Bible. It was exactly what I had asked God for and He was the only one that knew. This was the first time I really saw God move, and the first time I was in a place where I could learn how to hear His voice. Thankfully, He had just spoken in a very triumphant way and He had my attention.

As I read quickly through the comic book version of the Bible I attended another service. The jail services were held three times a week by three separate ministers, Mike Holsapple, Frank Ira with

*"Unchained Ministries,"*[8] and Dirus Dustin. They all had a different preaching style and it took some adjustment for me because this was not the kind of teaching I was use to through the Mormon Church I grew up in. The yelling did create a problem for me for a while but the truths that were spoken overshadowed the yelling and I began to feel the passion, hope, and love that these men were speaking to me and it became personal. The preaching was exposing my sins and challenging me to get up and do something about it. The message of repentance and remission of sins was distilling some hope into my life. I had yet to commit to making Jesus my Lord; however, I was on a journey towards God.

I got moved from a four man block upstairs to K block which was a 24 man block. It was in this block that I began confessing Jesus Christ as my Savior but had not made Him Lord. It was from there that I added depth to my experience with Jesus. This time in jail became part of the training for a calling and born again experience that did not come until years down the road, though.

In K block, I bunked with a man named Kerry Silvers. Kerry was incarcerated for using force in the commission of a robbery (strong arm robbery). He held a gun to another person's head and he is the one God used to lead me to a deeper knowledge of Him. He was a Biblical guide in my life for the next four months as I made my journey towards God's purpose for my life.

This is the guy that God chose to speak prophetic words into my life. In the winter months in 1997 from K block in a two-man cell, Kerry shared with me that God was calling me to be a leader of men like us. I would not know what this meant until 2007. Kerry was looking at life in prison and he struggled to accept that this was God's plan for his life. He was so intelligent that it was scary; however, the

---

[8] This is a nationally recognized prison ministry made up of mostly bikers

definition dumb smart may have been more fitting. He ended up escaping from prison and became one of Americas Most Wanted. His story has been featured on *"I Almost Got Away with It"* and *"Americas Most Wanted."* You can also read more about his story in his book *"American Refugee."*

Dirus Dustin with *"Free Indeed Ministry"*[9] is the one that brought me the message that I was lost and needed salvation and I did make a commitment to serve Christ while I was in jail. While Kerry Silvers, a despised and foolish man of this world, is the one the Lord used to expound scripture into my ear.

I served a full year in jail and at the time of my release from jail, I was physically fit and spiritually stuffed. My wife Brandy had divorced me while I was incarcerated. I was a twenty-seven-year-old single man who considered himself to be a Christian. I had no idea how to live a Christian life and no idea of what submitting to authority looked like. I found myself surrounded with those of the Pentecost and Holiness movement because they had invested in me and loved me while I was in jail.

My new life with Christ at that time reminds me of a story from my childhood. One night our family was planning to go out to eat at Long John Silver's. This was an exciting thing in our family because we did not go out to eat very often. The same evening, before we left for dinner, I received an invitation from the neighbor boys to ride bikes to their farm in the Guthrie Bottoms. This invitation was a big deal also because I had never been allowed to ride on the road. My parents always told me that when I turned eight I would be old enough to ride my bike on the road. I was overjoyed at the opportunity to finally ride my bike on the road with my friends.

---

[9] Free Indeed ministry is a prison ministry founded by Dirus and Kathy Dustin located in Bedford, IN

There was this hill called Guthrie Hill right at the beginning of our journey. For years we had sat at the top of this hill and dreamed of the day we would be allowed to ride our bikes down this hill. We were so excited we could not stand it, and as we approached the hill, we were filled with the excitement of this moment. The closer we got to the hill the harder we peddled and the further down the hill we got the faster we went.

This was the life for an eight-year-old like me. I thought this was freedom until I heard one of my friends screaming from behind me. I turned to look and he had crashed in the middle of the road, and as I turned back around, my handle bars began to shake uncontrollably and I found myself out of control just like him.

The next thing I knew, I was picking myself up out of a sand pile along the side of the road, battered and scared. In an attempt to get the attention of those riding ahead that didn't crash I let out load screams of pain, agony, and embarrassment. I will never forget going out to eat that night. I could hardly move and felt miserable. I have since learned that with freedom comes great responsibility.

When I was released from jail, I had the same earnest desire to peddle as fast as I could because I was so excited about the new life I had been introduced to. I thought every Christian was just as excited as I was. Talk about culture shock. I had no idea what I was about to face. I thought I had been set free but freedom is not being free from authority and the consequences of bad behavior. Being free is the willingness to come under authority and submit to those who are in the positions of delegated authority.

The area I failed, was still wanting to be over others when I had never learned how to come under authority. God will never allow people into anointed positions of authority until they can place themselves under authority and sit at the feet of Jesus until their due season.

This lesson was a necessary one for me to learn and would take me through a lot of heartache and pain to get me to the place I am today. I would be battered, bruised, and scarred, but eventually still end up rebelling against God by not submitting to his authority.

At the time, I blamed the Church for being imperfect with its legalistic doctrines that I felt cause division, but as I have grown up and matured, I have come to realize that it wasn't them; it was me. I was willing to call myself a Christian and I wanted Jesus to be my Savior. But what I was missing was Jesus as my Lord and the evidence of being a disciple.

I began this journey with Christ from jail and on fire and full of zeal, but the one doctrine that I had a difficult time accepting after my release was the doctrine of divorce and remarriage which commanded that I live as a single person because I had already been married. To be honest, at this time in my life I was unwilling to accept that Christ wanted me to be without a partner. I had no personal conviction from the Lord or the Bible that I could not re-marry as a new creation in Christ; however, I lacked the patience needed to wait on the Lord. In this way I was still worldly and I wanted what I wanted. This desire initiated by backsliding as a new Christian because I gave in to the lust of my flesh which led to many sexual encounters before I met my wife, Joy.

It didn't take long after I began to be sexually immoral for me to go back to smoking, drinking, and getting high. I tried very hard to wear my W.W.J.D (What Would Jesus Do) bracelet everywhere I went. I talked about God at the bars and began to use scripture to defend myself and justify my behavior. I went back to jail on several occasions for small things that year. I failed to follow up on court appearances, and as a result, there were several warrants for my arrest.

The only good that came from by backsliding was that I met my current wife, Joy, during this phase of my life. We crossed paths at several different bars before we became a couple. We decided to try and build a life together away from both of our hometowns, so we moved to Green County, Indiana. Our plans were to work and try to take care of my misdemeanor warrants that were mostly due to unpaid child support fees.

Joy had never been raised in Church. I knew that I needed to get back to reading, praying, and obeying God or else my future was going back to jail for good. Joy became pregnant and we were now faced with some tough decisions to make. We needed to get all this legal stuff behind us so we could provide a life for our child. I began going back to church but Joy wasn't ready. Eventually, she began to come with me, but her heart wasn't really there for Jesus, and I only wanted Jesus to fix my circumstances, I was using Him. She became pregnant by a rebellious loser and somehow fell in love with me and placed her confidence in her future husband.

We continued to attend church and I began serving inside the Church. I decided to give my court cases to the Lord. I committed to turn myself in two months before the baby's due date so that I would be out of jail for the birth. We saved enough money to pay our bills in advance for two months and Joy moved in with her mother back in her hometown while I was in jail. I spent 23 days in jail before I was released and then we returned back to Bloomfield and the church family we were committed to.

We made a commitment while we attended church to stop having sex and for five months we slept in separate bedrooms at separate ends of the trailer. We both had been married and divorced before so neither one of us had ever been married through the Lord. [10] We decided we should get married before the baby came and made an announcement to the Church that we were seeking the Lord in

---

[10] I do not support couples living together outside of marriage for any reason. We were in the wrong and this was done outside of Godly Biblical counsel.

marriage and would like to be married in the Church by the current Pastor Ron Stevens.

We believed this was the right thing to do; however, this was not how the Church felt. Divorce and remarriage is a controversial doctrine inside the Church and a doctrine that should be taken seriously but divided rightfully. I do not advocate divorce, but I do support restoration through a new birth in Christ Jesus, putting old things behind us so that Christ can do new things in and through us. I don't believe we should count men's sins against them after the cross. But I do agree that we will face the consequences of our sinful choices. Joy and I have had to go through many struggles as a blended family; however, these struggles are part of a testimony for how God can make miracles out of messes.

These are lessons that God allowed us to go through to teach us some valuable lessons for a later time on this journey. Not being able to marry inside our home church sent us on a journey over the next year that led us to backsliding yet again. I am in no way blaming anyone for our decision to distance ourselves from fellowship with God; it was our own fault.

Over the next year, I drifted from God, yet I was still desperate for God in my life. We visited over 30 Churches over the course of a year, and instead of coming under any one Church, we found reasons and excuses to not attend any Church. I would find fault in all and eventually I built a chapel inside our own home. I provided a religious symbol inside my home while developing a self-righteous attitude towards Christians and considered most of them to be hypocrites.

Eventually, since I couldn't find happiness or success in my attempt to live for God, I gave up striving for that Christian lifestyle and decided to go back to my old habits and friends. Joy never committed her life to God, so when I came home from work one day with a pack of smokes on the dash, she said, *"Yes!"* because she knew we were going back to our old lifestyle and this was what she had wanted all along. This is when I returned a second time to smoking, drinking, and getting high.

I made one final attempt to hold on to my religious experience when Joy and I went to a tattoo parlor. We were on a country cruise one weekend with the kids and I was drinking beer and decided I wanted a tattoo to express the recent bad experience I had in the Church.

I picked out a tattoo of a cross with the words, *"For Me"* written under it. Even though that statement was absolutely true, this act of marking me as righteous according to my standards was my rebellious spirit rising up in an ugly way. I am disgusted by that behavior to this day, but since that time I have learned a lot about how to handle disappointments within the church; however, since I didn't know how to deal with life's disappointments, I spent the next five years of my life as everything but a Christian husband and father.

## "CHRISTIAN"

Being a Christian is more than getting a religious symbol tattooed on your body, wearing a t- shirt with a religious expression, or attending religious services on regular basis. I have heard testimony after testimony of men in ministry that have served as leaders for years before receiving Jesus as Lord in their heart.

Many people are deceived in thinking that because they go to church, because they are in leadership, because they have a tattoo of the cross, or because they are generally a good person, they are a Christian. I was no different; my life had produced no evidence of me being a Christian. I was a criminal, a thief, and a liar that un-successfully stole the title Christian and attempted to use it to gain happiness and comfort for myself.

I was definitely on a search, but as I reflect back, what I was searching for more than anything else was for happiness and comfort. So, when I cried out for help from a bedroom and again from jail, I was sick, scared, and utterly lost and I was willing to try anything to obtain happiness and comfort. I have examined my heart, looked back at my journey towards Christ, and everything I did was based upon my desire to be happy and comfortable.

When I was on this search for happiness and comfort, I was reaching for things that were painless like a wife, job, and the American family dream. I had a deep need for peace, comfort, and a painless life and I was willing to give God a chance to provide that for me.

This explains why I used drugs, alcohol, and was sexually immoral. It also explains why I searched 30 different churches but settled on building my own chapel inside my own home. I was on a search for happiness, looking for something that would fulfill me and make me happy and comfortable. The problem with this search, though, is that it will never be complete during life on earth.

Only heaven can provide such perfection, and the truth is, on this side of heaven, it just isn't going to be that easy because we live in a world that constantly pressures us to perform. We are bombarded with pressure to rely on our own strength to control what happens in our life and to be tough enough to cope with life, all the while avoiding failure at all costs. Pressure like this drives us to believe that our performance is the measurement for success.

As a result, we invest our time, talent, and treasure seeking after the American dream of a happy family, a big house, and a prosperous career because in our culture this is the evidence of ultimate success. If we attain these things, then that means we have not failed. If we can just reach the American dream, then that means we have overcome the pressure the world puts on us to build our own happiness. Thus, in our search for such happiness and success, we are really on a quest for power.

Think about how you spend most of your time, when you put your talents to good use, and why you seek material gain. An honest analysis of where our true motivation originates will show whether we are using our time, talent, and treasure for our own personal gain of power to control happiness and success or if we are using them to glorify God and yield control to him.

We all value our time. It is so precious to us because we always feel like there is not enough time. But, what is the real reason that we value our time so much? Is it because our time here on earth is short so we need to make the most of it to glorify God and spread the Gospel? Or is it because we want enough hours in the day to complete our own to-do lists? In the same sense, we all strive to be good at something – a career or a hobby. But what is the underlying reason for our desire to be talented? Are we honestly striving to be more talented and skilled so we can better serve God? Or is it because we want a promotion?

The answers to these questions reveal where we are storing up treasure. If we use our time and talent for personal glorification, we are striving to store up treasures on earth that are fleeting and temporary, but God wants our time, talent, and treasure to be used for His glory and when we allow him to use us, we will be putting up treasure in heaven that is eternal.

The weakest power or influence we can rely on to be successful in life is our flesh. Our flesh includes our will power and our ability to please those around us. Our fleshly spirits deceive us into believing that we can control our own life with our own physical strength and by leaning on our own understanding. The influence of our flesh and its desire to be in control of our own happiness is not God's way for us. Rather, he desires for us to rely on His Spirit. Our willingness to yield control to Him is the true measurement of success here on earth. This was the ultimate lesson I had to learn to truly be transformed from criminal to Christian.

Looking to my flesh to perform was idolatry, and this sums up my first experience that began while I was in jail. I was introduced to

Jesus and I was interested in Him being my Savior and what He could provide for me, but I did not make Him Lord of my life. I was influenced by my fleshly spirit and led by my own will power and I did what needed to be done to get through jail.

Once I was released, I tried to control everything by my own strength and I leaned on my own understanding. This influence through my own will power made me happy and comfortable while I was in jail, but after I was out I could not keep the law in my flesh and I lacked the power to continue. I attempted to live for God without the spirit of God and *"the mind governed by the flesh is death..."* (Romans 8:6 NIV).

So what happened to me after I attempted to perform the best that I could and I still felt inadequate, I still hurt, and I still felt guilty? I was a man that had tried to keep the law of God but was a miserable man and my life became a wreck again. So what did I do?

I came in contact with another influence in my search for happiness and comfort--the spirit of the anti-Christ. This is a user spirit which expects God to change their circumstances, but God does not want to change our circumstances; he wants to change us. This spirit is no different than when we use people to get what we want. I was using Jesus to change my circumstances.

This influence convinced me I can smoke, do drugs, be sexually immoral and still love Jesus. The spirit of the anti-Christ used self-deception to keep me from seeing how corrupt my thinking really was so that I wouldn't find my new life in Christ. This is the same spirit that tells us that Jesus is the way to finding happiness and comforts.

No one ever told me that the Christian life would be easy and problem free, but I was deceived to believe that it was so. I thought I was something when I was nothing and I deceived myself into believing I signed up for a problem free life with Jesus. When trials and struggles came, I had little understanding of how to overcome and definitely wasn't happy and comfortable with these trials *"...you have been grieved by various trials, so that the tested genuineness of your faith—more precious than gold that perishes though it is tested by fire—may be found to result in praise and glory and honor at the revelation of Jesus Christ"* (1 Peter 1:6-7 ESV). God allowed these trials to come to reveal my heart to me.

Calling myself a Christian while attempting to live a happy and comfortable life was not what Christ was calling me to. I was called to suffer *"For to this you have been called, because Christ also suffered for you, leaving you an example, so that you might follow in his steps"* (1 Peter 2:21ESV). While living in my flesh and influenced by the spirit of the anti-Christ, I could not be obedient to Jesus. There was no way in the world that I was going to suffer for Him! Many times at this place on this journey I remember saying *"I would die for Jesus"* but I was unwilling to stop having sex outside of marriage for Jesus or stop doing dope for Jesus. I was unwilling to suffer because I did not like pain; it was too uncomfortable.

These influences, the spirit of the flesh and the spirit of the anti-Christ, are in this world to lead us to the truth about Christ, and God allows them to work in this world, but his motive for these influences are for us to come to the end of ourselves and our dependence on this world. Only then can Christ come and live in our heart through the Holy Spirit.

There comes a time in every person's life when they must make a choice to follow Jesus and make Him Lord. I was at a place in my life where I lived by the law in my flesh and it brought what the law was designed to bring, death.

Finding myself in another mess, I expected Jesus to clean it up; this was nothing more than a user spirit. There is no doubt that God wants to set us free and set his love upon us but we have to choose Jesus above everything and everyone else in order to truly be set free. Once I learned this lesson, my life began to radically change and only then was I able to fully surrender to Christ finally in 2005 at Organics Plus.

Since 2005, I have become a Christian who dies daily so Christ can live in and through me. In my new found life with Christ in me, it is not about my comfort; it is about persevering and enduring. I have to be willing to suffer for Christ because He suffered for me so that I could be free, *"For freedom Christ has set us free; stand firm therefore, and do not submit again to a yoke of slavery."* (Galatians 5:1ESV).

I am still learning how to live as a genuine Christian. I am willing to submit to the authority of God's Word and it is no longer a burden to suffer for His name. After becoming a Christian, the next step I had to take was learning how to be a disciple. Being a Christian is so much more than just saying a prayer and having a one-time experience where you surrender all to Him. Freedom comes from learning how to be a disciple of Christ everyday. Praise God, I AM FREE.

# -4-

# From Prophet to Disciple

*Christian?*
*The real question is,*
*Am I a disciple?*

*And He said unto them, "Follow me, and I will make you fishers of men."*

Matthew 4:19 NIV

I was almost ten years old in 1978 when we were returning home from a church conference and I told my mother that one day I wanted to be a prophet. Her response was, *"if you want to be a prophet, you will have to begin preparing now."*

I leaned back into my seat and prayed, "God, start preparing me to be a prophet."

At the age of ten, I had no idea what a prophet was or the sacrifice required to speak on God's behalf, but I believed that was what I wanted to do.

So, what is a prophet? A prophet is someone that is appointed by God. He stands in the gap between God and His people and delivers the message of God. On the other hand, a false prophet is someone that has not been appointed by God, but rather, has self-appointed themselves and assumes the authority to speak for God to the people. Before meeting Jesus at *Organics Plus* the latter was me, influenced and deceived by a spirit that cannot be a disciple of Jesus Christ.

So, what is a disciple? A disciple is a person who has trusted Christ for salvation and has surrendered completely to Him. He or she is committed to practicing the spiritual disciplines in community and reaching their full potential for Christ and His mission. On the contrary, a false disciple is someone that has an appearance of salvation but has not surrendered to Christ and is looking for a man to follow or men to follow him as he is on his own mission.

The difference between the two is that a prophet, also known as a messenger, is a position held by a person who was first a student, but a disciple is a position of a student that grows into a future messenger. Thus, no one can be a prophet (teacher) without being a disciple (student) first. The requirements of becoming a messenger for God cannot be obtained without completely surrendering to Christ and becoming His student as a disciple.

When I speak of the transformation of a prophet to a disciple, I am describing a person that is no longer driven by performance, titles, or self-exaltation. One lesson I learned on my discipleship journey that I hope others will learn too is that you must get over yourself before you can be a disciple of Christ. Jesus states this lesson simply, *"The student is not above the teacher...it is enough for students to be like their teachers,"* (Matthew 10:24-25 NIV).

## PROPHET

As I reflect back on my life, I see that a prideful spirit was at work in me. I allowed my pride to exalt me to positions that were not appointed or anointed by God. I believed I was something, when really I was nothing because I was seeking to be great on my own accord. Many people are affected similarly by pride. We will never succeed to reach such high and lofty expectations to be great, though.

We are deceived into believing that we are supposed to be great, but only God is great.

I always struggled with this type of pride in life. I felt like I should be the one that got the promotion. I tried hard to convince others why I should be in charge. And when I wasn't exalted to the place I felt I should be, I would blame those who I believed were standing in my way.

With every new phase of my life, I wanted to be the best. I always had the idea that God was going to do some exceptional thing in my life to make me great. I believed He was preparing and equipping me to do extraordinary work in the future and that I would receive recognition.

I lived life with this puffed-up attitude for a long time. I yearned for the day that I would be noticed for how great I thought I was. I wanted to be top dog in a pulpit at age ten, top dog on the ball court at age sixteen, and top dog of the drug market at age nineteen. When I was sent to jail in 1997 in Bedford, Indiana at age 28, I wanted to be top dog for God in jail, and then top dog at every church I attended after my release.

I thought everyone should listen to me, the next big prophet, the guy in charge. In 1998, I stood up in a jail service and asked everyone to pray that I receive the gift of prophesy by referencing 1 Corinthians 14:39 KJV *"...covet to prophesy..."* The problem with this attitude at this time was that I was seeking this gift out of selfish ambition, and scripture says *"Do nothing out of selfish ambition..."* (Philippians 2:3 NIV). I had not gone through any preparation that would qualify me to speak on God's behalf. And I was seeking the best gifts; this had to be for my own personal glorification.

I always wanted to be the one up front, or heard, and my way was always the right way and everyone else was wrong. This is how messed up my thinking was before becoming a disciple of Christ. I had the appearance of humility at times but my attitude was to think higher of myself than what my calling at the time actually was.

When we would visit different churches my focus wasn't on how I could serve in small ways. My thoughts led to me becoming the future Pastor, the guy that would come in and save the day. This led to many self-righteous experiences that ended in failure and for that I am glad. Through these many failures I have learned that God glorifies Himself, and it has nothing to do with me.

What Christ did *"in me"* at Organics Plus in 2005 led me into a disciplined and sanctified life. It was the decisions, changes, and growth that began to take place after I truly gave my heart to Christ that were evidence of a true commitment to Jesus alone.

All my previous experiences stopped at the cross but this power in Christ and Christ in me compelled me to take up my cross daily and follow Him. Salvation and the cross is not the end; it is the beginning. I am now His workmanship created in Him to do good works. I am so grateful and thankful because I was so broken and messed up in my thinking. I can't express enough the change that happened inside of me.

I knew I was genuinely changed because in that moment, Christ put an end to my old way of thinking. My pride was taken away and I didn't care if I preached or didn't preach. I didn't care if my past choices meant I could never lead in any Church or any job. This is when I became a disciple of Christ! I made up my mind that I didn't want to ever go back to my old life.

It was at this place that I chose Jesus above everything as the scriptures require *"If anyone comes to me and does not hate his own father and mother and wife and children and brothers and sisters, yes, and even his own life, he cannot be my disciple. Whoever does not bear his own cross and come after me cannot be my disciple."* (Luke 14:26-27 ESV). I was no good to anyone the way I used to be. I

David Louis Norris Jr.

was no good to my wife; I was a horrible father, and son. I was no good to anyone without Jesus and I finally knew it.

I would still have to shed a lot of flesh along this journey but I found a lasting relationship with Christ when it became Christ working in me. For the first time I realized I was sinning against God, which led to genuine repentance. I knew in my heart that the God I had sinned against had control of my life and my death. I was no longer in charge of my life and every time I attempted to take control from that moment, God reminded me that I had surrendered to His will.

What else changed? My attitude, I became teachable and I was truly thankful and grateful to God for His love that He bestowed upon me. I began to love Him and became willing to come under His authority. God had always loved me but I never really loved Him and that is why I couldn't submit and obey Him. Once I fell in love with Him, everything changed and this love led to obedience just as the scripture says *"Anyone who loves me will obey my teaching..."* (John 14: 22-24 NIV).

When the spirit of the flesh and the spirit of the anti-Christ failed me, I was ready to receive the new birth through the Holy Spirit. Jesus is what happened to me and changed me. Jesus is the influence that set me apart from the world for His purpose. I am powerless to please God without Jesus and the Holy Spirit living in me.

God sends the Holy Spirit to sin-sick souls. I was a sin-sick soul. When His spirit moved on my heart, the heart of an uncomfortable, hopeless, powerless, bruised, and broken man, my eyes opened to see the destruction of my choices. I was embarrassed and ashamed. I was mortified that I had tried sports, business, money, and drugs to find happiness and comfort.

The only way that I got through the pain and the guilt was through the blood and cross of Jesus Christ. The only way that I could

73

be forgiven and receive the grace of God was through the power of Jesus Christ and being born again through the Holy Spirit.

The spirit of the flesh says, "Keep up a good performance and you will live." The spirit of the anti-Christ says, "Try anything but Jesus first and you will be happy." The Holy Spirit says, "Jesus, Jesus, Jesus is everything you need."

I made my choice to be a disciple and follow Jesus. I love this song sung by Jeremy Camp *"Give Me Jesus."* This is the truth I want to share with the world.

### "Give Me Jesus"
Jeremy Camp

In the morning, when I rise
Give me Jesus.
You can have all this world,
Just give me Jesus.

When I am alone,
Give me Jesus.
You can have all this world,
Just give me Jesus.

When I come to die,
Give me Jesus.
You can have all this world,
Just give me Jesus.

# "DISCIPLE"

## STEPS OF DISCIPLESHIP

### 1. RECOGNIZE YOU ARE A SOLDIER

In 2006, I was learning to follow Christ. I was looking for a way to provide for my family and do something honorable. I decided I was going to sign up for the Army at age 37. I scored well on the Armed Services Vocational Aptitude Battery (ASVAB) but failed miserably on the background check. With two felony charges and exceeding the limit on misdemeanors, I did not qualify for the U.S. Army. One of the first lessons to learn on my quest to follow Christ was how to accept disappointments. I was rejected, but the spirit of truth let me know the U.S. Army was not where I was called; I was called to serve in God's Army.

The invitation from Paul in 2 Timothy was to join him as a good soldier. Paul told Timothy, *"Join with me in suffering, like a good soldier of Christ Jesus"* (2 Timothy 2:3 NIV). This image is the heart of discipleship and a great model for the teacher and the student walking into battle together.

Having the mindset of a soldier is a correct step in putting on the right attitude for battle *"Put on the whole armor of God, that you may be able to stand against the schemes of the devil"* (Ephesians 6:11ESV).

You must realize you are a soldier in God's army before you can become a true disciple, and in order to do that, you must first understand fully what a soldier in God's army does, what he thinks, how he feels, and what weapons he uses to fight for God's Kingdom and protect against the devil's power.

75

If you are a soldier in God's army, this declaration should remind you to live faithfully as a soldier of Christ each day.

## I AM IN THE LORD'S ARMY!

*I am a soldier in the army of my God.*
*The Lord Jesus Christ is my commanding officer.*
*The Holy Bible is my code of conduct.*
*Faith, prayer, and the Word are my weapons of warfare.*

*I am a volunteer in this army, and I am enlisted for eternity.*
*I will either retire in this army at the rapture*
*or die in this army;*
*but I will not get out, sell out, be talked out, or pushed out.*
*I am faithful, reliable, capable and dependable.*

*If my God needs me, I am there. If He needs me in Sunday*
*school, to teach the children, work with the youth, help adults*
*or just sit and learn He can use me because I am there!*

*I am a soldier; I am not a baby.*
*I do not need to be pampered, petted, primed up,*
*pumped up, picked up or pepped up.*
*I am a soldier.*
*No one has to call me, remind me, write me,*
*visit me, entice me, or lure me.*
*I am a soldier.*
*I am not a wimp.*

*I am in place, saluting my King,*
*obeying His orders, praising His name,*
*and building His kingdom!*
*No one has to send me flowers, gifts,*
*food, cards, candy or give me handouts.*

*I do not need to be cuddled, cradled,*
*cared for or catered to.*
*I am committed.*

*I cannot have my feelings hurt bad enough to turn me around.*
*I cannot be discouraged enough to turn me aside.*
*I cannot lose enough to cause me to quit.*

*When Jesus called me into this army, I had nothing.*
*If I end up with nothing, I will still come out ahead.*
*I will win.*
*My God has and will continue to supply all of my needs.*
*I am more than a conqueror.*

*I am a soldier in the army,*
*and I am marching claiming victory.*
*I will not give up.*
*I will not turn around.*
*I am a soldier, marching heaven bound.*
*Here I stand! I will not turn around.*

*Will you stand with me?[11]*

## 2. SIT, LISTEN, AND LEARN

My first step in being a soldier for God was to stop church hopping. I committed to just sit, listen, and learn. Although I was changed and this journey was different; I still struggled with pride, self-righteousness, and being judgmental. I still spoke out of turn, desired to be heard above everyone else, and attempted to figure things out in a way that made the most sense to me. I was still

---

[11] Adapted from the New Philadelphia, Ohio bulletin

attempting to explain myself but I was sitting, listening, and learning enough that I was able to count the cost of being a student.

I enlisted in God's army and I was committed to not quitting. This is an important point, we must recognize that we are an enlisted soldier in God's Army and the next lesson for us to learn is when to be still and hear God's voice for guidance.

Even though I was committed, I did struggle with sitting and staying put. In my struggle, I drove to see the man that first introduced me to the gospel, Dirus Dustin, to get counsel. I began to share my struggles by questioning what God was doing to *"MY LIFE."* There have been many divine appointments on my journey but only a handful of defining moments and this visit to see Dirus was one of those defining moments that would change me in a very significant way.

As I was running my mouth with my random thoughts Dirus stopped me and said these words to me: "David, I am going to tell you what I believe you need to do. I have never said this to you before because I didn't think you were ready for it but I believe you are ready to hear this" he paused, looked me straight in the eyes and said **"JUST SHUT UP."**

That sounds pretty harsh but for the first time in my life I shut up long enough to listen and my attitude has not been the same since. The power of being able to listen to a rebuke and receive it is amazing. Something else inside of me broke at that moment and I found myself receiving counsel that confirmed this wasn't *"MY LIFE"* any longer!

We need to be patiently listening to hear God's voice as scripture says *"Be still before the Lord and wait patiently for Him…"* (Psalm 37:7 ESV). Once we have committed to the Lord's Army, we are waiting on orders, we become teachable and learn the lesson of being still. We will hear God's voice for guidance and we will be more prepared to see the immediate needs of those closest to us.

## 3.  BE A TRUE, GENUINE WITNESS

Besides having Christ in my heart, I was alone on my journey. My family went to Church with me every now and then, but they were not seeking Christ like I was, so I was walking with Christ on my own. My family had to choose for themselves whether they wanted to walk their own journey with Christ or not because, *"What men think out for themselves, they never forget."[12]*

I was committed to keeping my mouth shut and allowing them to find their own desire to follow Jesus. One thing that those without Christ are looking for is a genuine power that produces evidence of something real. The only way to discover this power is to have been genuinely converted to Jesus Christ and Him alone. He is the Power.

My family had not yet come to accept Christ but their eyes were on me to see if I had genuinely changed.  They didn't read the Bible or attend Church every time the doors were open, so I had to present the Bible to them through my words and actions until they were ready to accept Jesus for themselves.

In September of 2006 after almost one year of being the Bible to my family, a revivalist came to Crossroads Community Church to minister. We committed as a family to attend every night. The first night my step-daughter, Shannon, and step-son, Cody, went forward and asked Christ to be their Savior.  The next night, Joy went forward and asked Jesus Christ to be Lord of her life.  The four of us were baptized together over the next few weeks.

Breanna was living with Brandy, my ex-wife, but was visiting with us more than ever due to a genuine change we had made in our

---

[12] Cosmo Lange

life. Breanna also accepted Christ and was baptized. We also were given custody of Breanna and she came to live with us.

With all this excitement happening inside our home my seven-year-old son, Caleb, began to ask questions and desired to have what his family had, a relationship with Jesus Christ that was genuine and real. Because he was so young, I talked with him and I searched the Word and I chose not to hinder him from accepting Christ as his Lord and being baptized. But instead, I accepted the responsibility to train him in the way he should go and through his confession of faith, hold him accountable and trust God to keep him.

The best way to win those closest to you is to be a true genuine witness *"But you will receive power when the Holy Spirit has come upon you, and you will be my witnesses..."* (Acts 1:8 ESV). This is not an easy task but one that I encourage you to be resilient in. Remember it took almost a year before my family made decisions to follow Christ *"Wait for the Lord; be strong and take heart and wait for the Lord"* (Psalm 27:14 NIV). Being genuine and real about the commitment you make to live for Christ will always lead to multiplication into the kingdom of God. It is God's desire that none be lost.

## 4.  LOSE WHAT POSSESSES YOU

If we are honest about our love for Jesus we should be growing. I was growing in my faith, but I was also being tormented by possession that had no eternal value. I was holding onto a lot of material possessions from my old life because they once held a lot of value to me.

A necessary part of living my new life in Christ was willingly putting the old life behind me *"Therefore, if anyone is in Christ, he is a new creation. The old has passed away; behold, the new has come"*

(2 Corinthians 5:17 ESV). Disposing of possessions that had a stronghold on me is part of how I became a new creation in Christ. Because of Christ these possessions were losing power over my life and their value was depreciating rapidly. Satan was being forced to loosen his grip.

I had made such a mess of my life that I had little energy to deal with the stuff I had accumulated so it had been sitting in our garage for a year. I had extra sets of appliances, trash compactors; grow equipment, tools, furniture, etc... tens of thousands of dollars' worth of stuff that had been packed into a garage.

I considered selling some things when times were tough but I felt guilty trying to sell what I gained illegally. My whole life had been manipulation and hustling, and I was over it. I asked God what He wanted me to do when I came across this scripture *"...It is more blessed to give than to receive"* (Acts 20:35 ESV). God put it on my heart to begin giving this stuff away. So my wife and I began to give as the Lord directed.

I started by having my Uncle Rick come and clean out all the left-over stock from Organics Plus. I had spent countless hours, weeks, months, and years of my life learning how to grow marijuana, sell marijuana, and advocate for the legalization of marijuana; it was time to put an end to the deception. Hydroponic equipment and supplies are not sinful or illegal when used properly; however, the hold they had on my life had to be dealt with.

Throughout our lifetime we make idols out of just about anything like cars, money, food, entertainment, people, etc... Scripture is clear that the Lord will not tolerate idolatry *"You shall not make for yourself a carved image, or any likeness of anything that is in heaven above, or that is in the earth beneath, or that is in the water under the earth"* (Exodus 20:4 ESV). Even seemingly good things in our life can become idols if we put them above God and spending time with Him. While celebrating and boasting your idols seems good at the time, it is a grave disservice to idolize anything or anybody. Our God is a jealous god and he commands us to have no other gods before him. As disciples, we must rid ourselves of idols. If we don't, God will destroy them for us, a lesson I learned the hard way.

I have had several cars, trucks, and motorcycles in my lifetime but I never loved a vehicle the way I loved my Dodge truck. This was the nicest truck I had personally ever owned. Looking back, I know that I idolized that truck because I loved it so much, it was all I thought about, talked about, and put my faith in. I was learning to love the Lord and the Lord was asking me to destroy some idols in life. He was asking me to give the truck to Dirus Dustin the founder of Free Indeed Ministry's.[13]

Over the next few weeks I told Joy what the Lord was asking me to do and how it didn't make any sense. I knew what God was asking but I was having a hard time understanding that God would ask us to give away our only vehicle.

What kind of soldier survives by keeping things that are not valuable for his survival? What kind of student would I have been if I heard God asking me to lose what possessed me but I wasn't willing to sit, learn, and listen to the lesson? This is where being a genuine follower of Christ will show what is most important to us. After seeking the Lord and desiring to please Him I left the altar of prayer and immediately called Dirus and told him that God wanted him to have my truck. I told Dirus, *"I will put the title on the dash, it is yours."*

We should admit that we North American Christians have been spoiled by materialism. And understand that this is to our own loss; we have relaxed and have become spoiled by easy living. Is eternal

---

[13] Free Indeed Ministries is a prison ministry founded by Dirus and Kathy Dustin and operates in Southern Indiana

life in heaven with Jesus enough for me? Are we evangelistic enough, zealous enough, broken enough, tried enough to be ambassadors that He will use today?

Jesus speaks about putting our hands to the plow and the one that looks back is not ready for God's call on His life, Jesus said to him, *"No one who puts his hand to the plow and looks back is fit for the kingdom of God"* (Luke 9:62 ESV). We can't look back with regret over the loss of possessions, but rather, we keep plowing, refusing to be mastered by this world of materialism. God is calling us all to a special task, *"Before I formed you in the womb I knew you, before you were born I set you apart..."* (Jeremiah 1:5 NIV). It is humbling and comforting to know that God has a plan for each of us. Don't get in the way of God's plan for you by holding on to possessions. Life is too short and there is too much work to be done for God's kingdom to let pride or idolatry rob you of blessings.


## 5.  BE OBEDIENT TO GOD

Being obedient to God and giving away our only means of transportation produced in me the desire to obey God at any cost. Falling in love with Jesus is a wonderful thing and it removes the burden of coming under His authority. So many claim to love God but will not obey Him. It was no longer a burden for me to throw down every weight that hindered my relationship with Jesus. I am still amazed at how much God loves me and this has made me extremely grateful for His sacrificial love that I want to model this for others to see.

I have always provided for my family but I had mostly done it through crooked means. My wife wanted me to get a job with good pay, set hours, and benefits. I wanted to learn to listen to those around me by being a servant to them and I desired to love God first and others second no matter how difficult this would be for me. God doesn't always ask us to do things that are pleasant. There are times when he asks us to go accomplish a small task that has little to do with the bigger task He is gradually leading us to accomplish. He does this so that we will develop an attitude of obedience even when it doesn't make sense to us.

God was always asking me to do things that didn't make sense to me. And it messed with the way I was use to handling what life dealt me. This created an attitude towards obedience and an understanding of scripture, *"For my thoughts are not your thoughts neither are your ways my ways, declares the Lord"* (Isaiah 55:8 ESV). Becoming obedient to His thoughts and His ways was crucial to understanding why the retail business had collapsed, money had been wasted, the truck was gone, and I had no job; I was down to nothing, but God was up to something. It was then I received a call from Dave Mallet, a friend I met while in Lawrence County jail in 1997. After our release we strengthened our friendship at Southside Seminary Church in Bloomfield, Indiana.

Dave was struggling in his faith and he worked an hour and forty-five minutes away in Indianapolis through the Carpenters Union. He owned a vehicle but needed a driver, he pulled some strings and got me a job in the union working at Lucas Oil Stadium. This was what my wife always wanted-- a job with good pay, set hours, and benefits. I couldn't deny the timing of this opportunity. My first day of work was on November 1, 2006 one full year after I had cried out to God at Organics Plus.

With no truck and a good paying job the Lord put on my heart that I no longer had any use for my Haulmark tool trailer. The goal was not to lose something else that had possessed me but to be an obedient witness to someone I loved. I had a friend who needed the trailer, and I knew God could use the gift as an opportunity for my family and me to build a testimony for Jesus, so the family and I filled up the trailer with construction tools and delivered it to Tim Bridwell, a partner I worked with in the construction industry. He was not a believer in Jesus or any religion but on Christmas morning 2006, before dawn, we knocked on his door and said *"Merry Christmas!"*

I had my brother Brian pull the trailer with his truck. Brian could not understand how we could be in such financial trouble and just give all these tools away. Tim could not believe it either and he thought for a long time there was a catch. This simple act of obedience slowly worked on Tim's heart. Tim said *"if God is real I believe it because you are different."* Through acts of obedience the Lord has let us know that you cannot put a price tag on a soul. One day, I hope to see Tim at an altar giving his life to Jesus.

In 2007, after the job came to an end at Lucas Oil Stadium, I spent the next few weeks seeking God's direction and found myself working at several different power plants. Even though this is what my wife had wanted our whole marriage, for me to get a good paying job, steady hours, and benefits, my heart was torn. I wanted to please my wife but my heart was to work for the Lord full-time. I desired to do more than make a living with my tool belt. I wanted to please my family, but I wanted to please God more.

After the power plant season came to an end, I was sent to a job close to home working in Bedford. My heart was on full throttle in searching out God and His ultimate purpose. I felt there was more that God wanted me to be doing. One morning before I left for work I got on my knees in the driveway, car door open, and cried out to God this prayer. *"God if this job is not exactly where you want me to be at this moment please shut the door."* I got into my car and headed to work. With no rumors and nothing out of the ordinary, my foreman called me over to his truck and handed me a hand-written check with my pay up through the rest of the day and told me that they would have to lay me off and offered no explanation.

At first, I was upset. It was not until after I left that I understood the fullness of what had just happened. God spoke and answered my request from that morning's prayer. This led to a deep yearning in my soul and this became my plea. *"If not this God then what?"*

We must do as scripture says and have complete trust that when we follow His Word, he will take care of us. The Lord promises, *"Trust in the Lord with all thy heart and lean not on your own understanding; in all your ways submit to Him and He will make your paths straight"* (Proverbs 3:5-6 NIV) Obedience is a result of loving God and is the key to a successful life. Do I want to leave a footprint on this planet for others? Obeying God is in our best interest. I would not be where I am today without being obedient and you will not be in a place for God to bless your life without obedience. And you and I will never do anything good in this life without first being obedient to God. Obedience will produce a life that glorifies God.

## 6.  GLORIFY GOD WITH YOUR LIFE

Being laid off, brought me into a deeper search for God and His next assignment. At this point in my journey, I began to desire to be used by God in little ways which was the opposite of how I used to think. It was at this time that I began to understand that discipleship develops from the willingness to minister to one person at a time. This is when I began to develop the idea for Heaven Nevaeh Healing Center, a home mission's discipleship ministry.

Once I gave my life, treasure, talent, and time to the Lord, they no longer belonged to me anymore. Giving myself to the Lord first and others second is what I did with my life by becoming a disciple of Jesus Christ and He was calling me to make disciples and start a ministry for men that are just like me.

Before I could go to work doing the great commission for Christ, *"Go and make disciples of all nations…"* (Matthew 28:19 NIV), I had to come under and remain under authority and become a disciple (student) myself. The way God cleared the path in preparing me and my family to follow Him into the harvest fields is exciting; however, not everyone is called to work in the church or plant a nonprofit ministry. But we are all called to glorify God with our life and this is exciting. How can you glorify God in your chosen vocation? You may be called to stay put or step out in faith. Either way, you have a mission field so remember to put God first above everything else and you will bring glory to Him every day of your life wherever you have been called to serve.

I am *"Free at Last"* because I have received the call of the great commission and have chosen to be a student of the Lord. In the next chapter you will see how God took a player and turned him into a preacher.

# -5-

# From Player to Preacher

## *Is God's desire for my life good enough for me?*

*"Ponder the Path of your feet; then all your ways will be sure"*

Proverbs 4:26

Abraham Lincoln once gave the advice, *"Be sure you put your feet in the right place, then stand firm."* This advice refers to being steadfast in the path you choose to take in life. Our choices do not always line up with God's desire for our lives, though.

God's word is a guide to acquiring His desire for our life. Thus, we cannot know where to plant our feet and stand firm until we read His word. When we do not read His word, our choices are the result of stubbornness instead of being steadfast. These types of choices lead to ultimate failure because we are attempting to do something that wasn't God's desire for our life all along.

Such failure does not leave us lost, but rather, it leads us to being steadfast if we choose to learn from the failure. In order to do so, we must continuously examine the path we are on by asking the questions, *"Am I sure of what God wants my life to be? And if I am sure, do I trust God enough to stand firm in that path?"*

Before Christ, I was a player in many ways. I did not give careful thought to the paths my feet were on and this kept me from being steadfast and making choices that aligned with God's desire for my life. My heart was deceptive so I ignored what God wanted for me. As a result, I had to learn the hard way that my desires were full of stubbornness and selfish ambition, which were not God's desires for me. Instead, I created my own desire for my life and I chose to live that dream on my own.

The dream I had for my own life failed and it took years for me to realize that the dream I was chasing was not God's plan for my life at all. But even still, God uses our past experiences so we can learn from them and help lead others to Him.

The desires and passions that we chase on our own accord are often met with failure, and as a result, what we think our life should be is not what our life becomes. When life does not go as hoped or planned, disappointment, bitterness, and resentment can take root in your heart, which is what happened to me when my dream ended in utter failure. In my life the disappointment, resentment, bitterness and feelings of rejection were the result of my failed dream of being the best basketball player I could be. Others may have a similar dream of being the best *"something."* When a desired status is not achieved, people will most likely experience the same rejection that I experienced. We don't have to let our dreams end in such despair, though, even if we are rejected.

When we fail and our dreams die, God helps us learn from that failure so we can help others. Sometimes we have to experience the failure so we can use the lesson learned through it all to lead others to God. Realizing this helped me understand that the dream I was chasing so long ago, even though the initial dream died, it still has hope of a good outcome because I am now using that past experience to glorify God and help people live their dreams for Him.

As a preacher, I am now involved in people's lives in ways that I would have never imagined. I never thought I would be a preacher, but my experiences from the failures of my life have given birth to some of the greatest opportunity to show others the path to God's desires and their dreams for this life. I point them to God and His way. I steer them clear of the mistakes I made. I teach them to stand firm, and when they achieve their dream, I am blessed to have had a small part in the process.

It took me years to get to this point, though. I could not be as effective of a preacher if it had not been for my basketball career and the heartache it caused me. Basketball was how I defined my identity for most of my youth, but my path of destructive choices can be traced back to my high school basketball experience. My story is just one of many that demonstrate how life does not go as planned when we choose our own paths and dreams rather than the ones God desires for us. But my story also shows that there is hope even when our life turns out differently than expected. Perhaps no one who knew me as a youth would have guessed that God could take a player like me and eventually call him to be a preacher, but with God, anything is possible.

## THE PLAYER

Growing up in the heart of Indiana basketball, I quickly developed a strong love of the game. I was entrenched in basketball fever so my intense desire to play seemed only natural. I watched basketball greats like Kent Benson, Isaiah Thomas, Keith Smart, Landon Turner, and of course the greatest coach, Bobby Knight, and dreamed of playing ball just like them.

I was raised in southern Indiana near French Lick, the hometown of Larry Bird, a small-town Hoosier boy who made it to the National Basketball Association and led the Boston Celtics to three NBA titles. I also grew up with and was teammates with Damon Bailey, who holds the record for most points scored in a high school career in the state of Indiana and who earned All-America honors playing for the Indiana Hoosiers.

From as far back as I can remember I wanted to be as successful as all of these well-known Indiana players because they were my role models. It was no surprise, then, that from a young age all I wanted to do in life was play basketball.

As a child I played every chance I got. I would shoot ball on anything that had a rim and was within a two mile radius of my house. From the nicely paved church parking lot, to the goal attached to the side of a barn with a dirt surface, I would play. I wore the hide off of many basketballs, and I cannot even count the hours I invested in practicing.

I was a skinny kid that was always taller and faster than the other kids in my class. I grew up playing Biddy Basketball, Boy's Club, and organized school ball. One of my fondest memories was my sixth grade year when we won the Biddy Basketball League championship. Out of all my years playing basketball, this was the only season that my father coached my team, and our relationship was great. As I grew older, my love for basketball grew while my relationships with authority figures began to deteriorate.

As I have mentioned in previous chapters, my rebellion against authority led me down the path of destruction, but I have not yet shared in detail what initiated the rebellion. My rebellion was strongly influenced by the sport I loved more than anything else. There are commonly rooted issues and events that trigger rebellion. For me, the injustice of my dreams not coming true became one of the root issues in my life that led to deeper and darker sin.

Basketball became an idol, a false god in my life. I worked hard, and depended on the ball to be my savior, but my idol let me down and did not produce the happiness, comfort, or stardom I longed for. ⸢he end, I was left with an unfillable hole in my heart. I attributed ⸢ure as a player to my parent's faith, but I was also a victim of ⸢ss that is common to many kids that have been hurt within the sports culture in general. In return, I was filled with bitterness and rejection which began to fuel bad choices.

My experience with the injustice that can come through youth sports began my freshman year at Bedford North Lawrence High School. Since I transferred to BNL from Oolitic Jr. High, I was not a part of the clique that came in from Bedford Jr. High who had been playing together since they were nine-years-old. I had to wait for my opportunity to shine because these players were given priority due to their history playing together.

This is when I experienced sports and favoritism for the first time in my young life. Coach Flynn was the freshman coach and he had his favorites. Coach Flynn didn't give me the opportunity to play on the first team roster until other players began to quit or perform poorly. I spent most of the season sitting on the bench as a second string player. Todd Browning, a teammate witnessed the disappointments from my freshman year and wrote in an article to Hoosier Basketball *"He seemed bitter, and began to act out, and his slide was painful to watch."*[14]

I took advantage of the opportunity when it finally came and played hard to prove to the coaches and my teammates that I should have had more playing time all season. I finished the year in the starting line-up, but the injustice of that freshman year affected me greatly.

Off the court, I was ostracized by my teammates, and I assumed it was because I was raised in the Mormon faith. I began to act out in order to be accepted by my peers, who were not Mormon. This was one of the reasons that drove me to quit church. I thought it would help me to fit in. I wanted to be accepted desperately so I began to do stupid things. I quickly developed a reputation for being wild and doing crazy things.

---

[14] www.hoosierbasketball.wordpress.com

My sophomore year was a good year, I played junior varsity and dressed varsity. We went 19-1 as a JV team and towards the end of the year, I received some playing time at the varsity level, but not as much time as most people thought I should have been getting. I had a good year with school and grades. I was still accepting challenges to do wild and crazy things, but I wasn't doing it in a way that would get me in trouble. It was mostly just fun stuff to draw attention to myself while the real problems were surfacing at home with my parents.

My junior year was a pivotal year in changing my attitude and future career as a basketball player. My rebellion became more outward than inward during that year. I was so frustrated at not being a starting player on the team, and this frustration made me very unstable.

No one knew when I would lash out and do something stupid just to get attention; I might talk back to a teacher or pick a fight with a classmate. I was always chewing tobacco, risking getting caught and suspended at any moment. But when I was on the court, I was in my element.

One of the reasons I did not start was because the coaches could not depend on my eligibility due to behavior and academics. The fact that I was not starting games and the feeling of rejection was fueling me to act out. I really struggled with the lack of playing time. Some say if there had been a state award for best sixth man, or points per minutes played, I would have won that award hands down. I could score double digits in just minutes after entering the game. And anytime the game was going down to the wire I was always put on the court to secure the victory.

For a young man who spent his every waking hour wanting to play basketball, not playing nor receiving the recognition of my talent, was hard for me. My parents tried to encourage me, but I blamed them for my failing basketball career. Because of the Mormon faith, I was never able to participate and showcase my ability in

Amateur Athletic Union (AAU) because Sunday was a day of rest and most of the games were played on Sunday.

After my junior year, I really just gave up. In my opinion, there were several other players in the starting rotation that did not deserve to be starting or even be on the team. I worked hard every year trying to secure a spot that my talent and ability deserved. It just seemed like the only thing I got noticed for was bad behavior, so that was what I focused on the summer before my senior year.

When I started my senior year there was a big part of me that wanted to live right and stay out of trouble and play ball. I knew I had made a lot of mistakes and bad choices, but I wanted to do better. The coach didn't make me feel wanted or accepted on the team, so I battled with whether chasing my dream was worth it or not. In the past I knew that even when I wanted to do well, I could really screw things up in a hurry without even meaning to. Try-outs came and I was still not eligible because of my grades from the semester ending my junior year. But when grades came out at the end of the first nine weeks, I was eligible so Coach Bush, the varsity coach, gave me a chance.

After my first night of try-outs Coach Bush threw me my practice jersey but that did not mean I would get to play. That was something I would have to earn by staying out of trouble, and I knew that. The first week or two of practice was horrible for me because Coach would not use me in any of the lineups. Looking back, I believe he was only testing me to see how I would respond to such treatment. I was not very motivated because I felt everything was being stacked against me yet again.

I was ready to quit, and I thought that was what Coach wanted me to do as well. I felt that all by past mistakes were being stacked up against me even though I desired change. I wanted to be a part of this team more than anything else, but I felt like I was of no value to Coach. In my frustration, I attempted to reach out to him for help. I stayed after practice one night and told him that I may have to quit because my girlfriend could be pregnant. He didn't have much advice or reaction, only disgust. I wanted him to say, *"Don't quit we need you,"* but that didn't happen.

Just a few days later I was in the lunch room working on homework. I was really taking my school work seriously to show Coach I wanted to play. While I was working on an assignment, Rusty, the starting center on varsity, approached me and asked me to skip the rest of the day with him. My first reaction was no; I did not want to throw away everything I had worked so hard for. I told him no on several occasions, but I folded under the pressure this time. This decision altered the course of my life in a major way.

We left school because Rusty wanted to avoid taking a test until he was better prepared. With no plan and nothing to do, we were left to our own destruction. We decided to go visit my girlfriend at another high school.

While we were there, a confrontation took place between me and her ex-boyfriend, Chuck. Before I knew it about 50-100 students had gathered against us in support of Chuck. We quickly realized we were in over our heads when the hall monitor intervened and we were escorted to the office where they took our names and contacted BNL authorities.

We were in trouble and there was no way out. I decided I wasn't even going to attempt to defend myself or beg for another chance. Instead, I pleaded for Rusty to be allowed to remain on the team. I took full responsibility for my actions and explained that Rusty had a doctor's appointment and I was giving him a ride but wanted to stop at Bloomington North High School. Rusty was able to get a Doctor's note from his aunt and was suspended for one pre-season game. I was immediately dismissed from the team, and I pretended that I was okay with what had happened. But I was really torn up inside, worse than I had ever been.

The first game of the year for BNL boys' basketball was at Scottsburg, IN. I decided to go after I had already been drinking and smoking pot. After the game I decided that I wanted to see my ex-teammates. So I waited out by the bus for them to all come out of the gym. I was drunk and began crying, getting really loud and emotional until Coach Bush came out and told me to leave or he would have me arrested.

I had played the tough guy routine all the way up to that night and then I lost it. I had lived my life to play basketball. I went to school to play ball, and I attended class because of ball. Being a basketball player was the best thing in my life. This was the only thing I ever attempted to stay out of trouble for. I didn't want to mess this thing up, but I had. Basketball was what I lived and breathed for, and suddenly it was taken from me and the reality of it being gone had truly set in.

Before Christ, this was a part of my life that I was not comfortable talking about. I had dealt with people's opinions and what if scenarios ever since I was kicked off the team my senior year in 1986. I was a talented and gifted player that had potential to play at a Division I university but instead became the epitome of failure in Lawrence County.

I spent this entire season and the next 20 years of my life listening to everyone tell me how stupid I was and how good we could have been if I had remained on the team. We were already really good and ranked in the top ten in the state. It was after I was dismissed from the team that I began to use drugs and alcohol to cope with the destruction of my dream.

I let this event shape my life for the next 20 years before finally being set free. The unfillable hole in my heart from basketball could only be filled with Jesus Christ. Not until 2007 did I truly find freedom from my failed dream of playing basketball.

## "THE PREACHER"

On my way to becoming a preacher, there were many times I had to face my past of bad decisions and rejection. Hurting people hurt people, and I hurt a lot of people. There have been times when facing my past was a struggle and it will be the same for you too. Forgiveness is something that every man wants to receive, but it is also what every man needs to be willing to give to others. There are some people that will never forgive the hurt we have caused them, but we are not responsible for how they view us; we are only responsible for the forgiveness we show to those who have hurt us.

Yes, I hurt a lot of people in my lifetime and being constantly reminded of my abilities and potential by people in the Bedford community in the last 25 years has hindered my freedom. Yes, I let the community and my teammates down. For that I am deeply sorry, but I can no longer live thinking about what could have been. No one can change what happened, but we all have the choice to move on. That is what I chose to do and I hope others will to.

In 2007 I began to desire to be used by God in little ways which I had never thought before. My life had been sending a message of failure for twenty years, and it was time my life sent a better message. When I realized that, I began to understand that discipleship develops from the willingness to minister to one person at a time.

At that time, I began to develop the idea for *"Heaven Nevaeh Healing Center"* a discipleship ministry. My vision was to create a home for the lost to come, live, and learn about Jesus. My family and I began to seek the Lord on how we could work with men like myself and also keep our children safe and our home secure.

This quest led me to the Old Valley Mission Church in the Guthrie Bottoms where I wore the hide off of many basketballs. I began praying for this property which consisted of 17,000 sq. ft.

God gave us the location for the ministry, which meant I had to learn how to be a minister. I began to research how other discipleship ministries were founded and I learned there is so much more than just naming it and claiming. It took four years for us to gain possession of the property. God used that time to prepare us for the work ahead of us by teaching us the first lesson – waiting.

Before becoming a preacher of righteousness, a person must first experience a genuine call to follow Christ and submit to him. Just as the Bible states, *"For by grace you have been saved through faith. And this is not your own doing; it is a gift of God"* (Ephesians 2:8 ESV), the disciple must answer the Lord with faith. The call will not guarantee a better life but will require one to lay down his life. Before I could go to work doing the great commission of making disciples for Christ, I would have to come under authority and remain under authority. The way God cleared the path in preparing me and my family to follow Him into the harvest fields is exciting.

In the same summer of 2007 I woke up early in the morning with an impression from God on my heart. God was asking me to do two things specifically that morning. First, I was to drive to Oakland City University-Bedford (OCU-B) and apply to go back to school. Two, after I completed that I was to go to the Bedford Public Library and check out a book on Martin Luther King Jr.

The strange things about this request were that (1) I thought I was too old to go back to school; (2) I had no idea what I was supposed to study; (3) How in the world could we afford this; (4) I knew nothing about Martin Luther King Jr. except he had a dream.

I stopped at my wife's work and told her the two things God was asking me to. Part of me expected her to express my same concerns, but her response rattled me when she said, *"If that's what God wants, you better go."* When husband and wife come together with one mind for God and put him first, there is nothing like it!

99

I arrived at OCU-B with my uncertainties. The first thing I noticed was that there were many students who were older like me. The second thing I took note of was that it was a Christian College and they offered Theology as a major to study. As I doubted, He reassured, and as I questioned, He confirmed. I quickly realized it was God's desire for me to go back to school. I had no idea how we would survive financially while paying for college, so we grew in our faith and trust in Him alone. Our new slogan became *"If it's God's will, He will pay the bill."*

After doing everything needed to begin the enrollment process I was on my way to the library to get a book on Martin Luther King Jr. I began to read about the injustices of slavery and the shear resilience of a group of people fighting for freedom through a non-violent approach. It rattled me to the core because freedom from a sinful past had been my nemesis for so long.

The comparisons to slavery and bondage and my need for freedom were real but small in comparison to the injustices forced on the Negro people. It made my problems seem so insignificant but gave me hope and a method towards healing. And it is this civil rights movement of freedom that inspired the title of this book *"Free at last, Free at last, Thank God almighty we are free at last."*[15]

God would use OCU-B and Martin Luther King Jr. to confirm that I was called to be a preacher and I was finally where I was supposed to be. He gave me the opportunity to start my studies, and he also showed me the place I was called to preach and minister at the Church and Parsonage in Guthrie Bottoms. But it was a four-year journey of preparation before God revealed the truth of his promise.

After being a student for only a few months, I was asked to fill the position of OCU-B Chaplain. This was a great opportunity to become a spiritual leader among the students and staff. I had to wait

---

15 Martin Luther King Jr., I Have a Dream: Writings and Speeches That Changed the World

for the start of the second semester to become the official Chaplain. I was required to submit to the Dean and lead monthly chapel services that were already on the semester schedule.

The first Chapel service that I performed my official duties happened to be MLK Day, a nationally recognized holiday in honor of Martin Luther King Jr. The timing of this first Chapel was God's sovereignty confirming that my life was finally being led by the spirit and not by my own selfish desires.

To be called by the Lord as a messenger and disciple maker requires many tests. Tests are important because they reveal to us our true motives by providing opportunities to go through the fires of preparation and sanctification. In these tests we also find healing from our past failures.

My very first test as Chaplain came within the first month. I was implementing a daytime chapel service once a week. I scheduled it at a time that would be the most convenient for all students and staff. I spent a fair amount of time preparing, putting up flyers, and personally inviting people to attend. When the first service came, not one person showed up. There are many thoughts that go through a person's mind when he or she plans an event that no one attends. Feelings of failure, abandonment, and rejection are all real emotions that the devil uses to get us to quit.

The test, though, is in how we react and respond to the circumstance. In these moments of trial, we must stay focused on what pleases God and respond in the way that He wants us to respond. The Lord put on my heart a message to preach that day, so I preached the message I had prepared for the Lord, even though no one else came to hear it. I believe God was testing me in several ways when no one showed up. First, God wanted me to stand firm in my faith. Second, He was asking me *"Are you looking for a following, an audience, or do you really want to please me?"* Third, He reminded me that I must be willing to minister to one person at a time.

I have learned through many experiences that this reflection from Oswald Chambers holds true "If you are going to be used by God, He will take you through a number of experiences that are not meant for you personally at all."[16] I experienced this when I received a phone call during a BNL basketball game. A teenage boy had decided to escape the authority of his mother by jumping from the vehicle while it was traveling 65mph down the highway.

He was life-lined to Indianapolis and I was asked to go and minister to him when he woke up. When I arrived, I spoke to him briefly because he wanted nothing to do with me. I decided to spend the night in the hospital chapel praying for him and his mother. To this day I personally did not get to see the impact that my prayers had on this family, but God called and it wasn't supposed to be about me.

I was again tested when I was asked to lead our county's largest prayer vigil. Once again it was after a BNL girls basketball game when we received a call that four local teenagers had been involved in a devastating accident. Two lost their lives and two were life-lined to Indianapolis and unresponsive. The two survivors were both starters on the BNL girl's basketball team. I was asked by our local Church to go and pray over the two girls and support the families. We took prayer blankets with us and laid them over each girl as we asked God to heal their broken bodies.

The following Monday the Varsity Coach approached me to organize a prayer vigil for his team and our community. The school board of Lawrence County gave us full authority and access to the High School gymnasium and to preach healing through our Lord Jesus Christ. My return to the basketball court of BNL was not as a player but as a preacher of righteousness.

Now that I have been called to be a preacher, God has set me free from the failure of being a player. And the message I send to all

---

[16] Oswald Chambers *"My Utmost for His Highest"* Page November 5

is this: We can't live in the past but we all must face the past. So as a preacher, I want to help everyone find freedom from past failures. When people ask the *"What if's"* that serve as a reminder of injustice and failure, we have to be real with our response. People have always asked me if I had not been kicked off the basketball team would BNL have won the State Championship. I have heard many opinions to this question but here is the truth from my perspective:

"No, I was not a team player but one looking to fulfill my own dreams. My desire was selfish and God never blesses selfishness. My being on the team would have hindered the unity of the team. I believe it was God-ordained that I be cut for the sake of the team. I had lost my way and God's Sovereign justice was put on display. It is now my duty to help others learn from my failure."

Although we are all affected by injustice and failure, we cannot stay there. For many years I lived my life blaming God, man, and allowing rejection to bury me in self-pity. I have no excuse for the way I handled what life threw at me. I responded incorrectly and reacted wrong and I take full responsibility for my own behavior. I wasted my God-given talent by putting my faith in a ball and my hope in men who had no power to save me.

Without Christ coming into my life and calling me to be a preacher I would have never been set free from my past failures. I understand not everyone will be a preacher, but all of our lives send some kind of a message. What kind of message is your life sending?

I am *"Free at Last"* and I compel you to follow God's desire for your life. Whatever has happened to you that is seemingly unfair, unjust, or unethical, give it to Jesus and allow Him to bring your dreams to life through someone else. The promises of God are true and the desire of God for our life is much more fulfilling than if we follow our own selfish desires.

# -6-

# From the
# "High Times" and Amsterdam
# to the "Holy Bible" and Israel

## *It's 4:20, Your call.*

*"Immediately they left their nets and followed him"*

Matthew 4:20 ESV

In the drug culture, *"4:20"* refers to the time to get high and was a phrase I responded to many times when I identified with that culture, but now that phrase represents a new calling from God.

The subtitle of this chapter, *"It's 4:20, Your Call"* is a promise that God shared with me from Matthew 4:20. In this passage, Jesus called the disciples to follow Him and their response was, *"At once they left their nets and followed him."* When Jesus called them, they walked away from their livelihood without hesitating, even though fishing was their entire identity. They willingly chose to leave the culture they identified with and follow Jesus. We all have the same opportunity to respond to God's call and follow Him, but the first step is defining our identity in Him.

We spend so much time trying to discover who we are, and it is during this search to find our identity that we are influenced by many different peer groups, sometimes good and sometimes bad. Because of our human nature, we have an innate desire to belong and to have friends to share life with. It is so important for us to feel connected to others that at times we may join a certain peer group or culture to fulfill that sense of belonging only to realize after a short time, that is not where we truly belong. In my case, that is how I became involved in the drug culture, searching for my identity as well as a place to belong, and responding to the calling of my surroundings.

Whether we notice it or not, our culture calls us to belong to it through the people we listen to, the books we read, the media we consume, and the way we spend our time. Each day, we make decisions based on these callings in order to feel connected to something greater than ourselves, but when we focus on earthly callings, we will continuously struggle to fit in. As a result, we dream about our ideal identity and desire to find a culture to identify with, but only God can provide us with a clear and secure understanding of who we are.

When I committed to follow Jesus, I placed my identity in Him and He placed His identity in me. He taught me who I was and what I was to do. Responding to God's calling and finding my identity through Him ultimately set me free. But like most people, I first had to make several mistakes answering the call of the culture I felt connected to before I could answer God's call to follow Him.

As I share my struggle with defining myself through the drug culture, I ask that you think about what calling you are responding to in order to create your identity. Who are you trying to be and where are you trying to belong? If you do not already have a solid understanding of your identity in God, I pray my story will help you find the courage to answer God's calling for you. Once you let go of the need to identify with your culture, and instead, form your identity in God, you will experience the promises of God in miraculous ways.

## "HIGH TIMES" and AMSTERDAM

Living my life independent of God led me deeper into the drug culture. I thought this was the lifestyle I was called to be a part of, so

I climbed the corporate ladder of the drug industry by owning several businesses as a front for my drug-dealing lifestyle. I felt stuck, but I also felt an intense need to pursue this path in life.

My ultimate goal was to visit Amsterdam, Holland, the marijuana capital of the world where marijuana is legally sold in coffee shops and openly accepted. People come from all over the world to see, buy, and smoke the best bud and hashish in the world. This was the Mecca of my culture and became my dream and desire for life. I was searching for who I was and where I belonged, and I believed Amsterdam would have answers for me.

During my life as a drug addict and dealer, I subscribed to a monthly magazine called *"High Times"* founded in 1974 by Tom Forcade. This publication is devoted to and advocates the legalization of cannabis and offers its view on a wide range of topics including politics, activism, drugs, sex, music and film. *"High Times"* has long been influential in promoting the legalization and use of marijuana.

There was no question I was addicted to this lifestyle. I served this Idol of *"High Times and Amsterdam."* I wore the T-shirts, read the propaganda, and shook my fist at authority demanding my right to be free. I hoped and dreamed to visit Amsterdam one day, sit in a coffee shop and get baked on some of the best bud in the world. Each month *"High Times"* and the vision of going to Amsterdam not only fueled my intense desire to belong to the drug culture but at least 500,000 other people as well.

Under the influence of *"High Times"* I went from being a closet grower of marijuana to becoming involved in professional growing operations. After my friend was arrested for federal cultivation charges and my out-of-state operation was shut down, I invested everything I had left into selling the products and equipment to assist people in growing marijuana by opening my own store *"Organics Plus."* At that time, I thought marijuana should be legalized and that drug use was an individual's choice. These ideas, goals, and ambitions came directly from the seemingly overall cultural acceptance of drug abuse that I had identified with.

The drug culture that I belonged to advocated strongly for the legalization of marijuana and has been quite successful. The number of U.S. states that allow medical use of marijuana is 23 plus the District of Columbia. In addition, Alaska, Colorado, Oregon, and Washington have approved legally taxing and regulating marijuana. [17]

The drug culture has been at war with the federal government since the 1980's when President Ronald Reagan declared *"War on drugs."* Since July 2000 the DPA has been the nation's leading organization working to end this war on drugs. The supporters of the DPA believe that *"the war on drugs is doing more harm than good."*[18]

Some of the statistics from the war on drugs are astounding and reflect the massive support this culture has gained over the years. In 2013 the U.S. spent $51,000,000 fighting illegal drugs; 693,482 people were arrested for a marijuana law violation; 2,220,300 were incarcerated in federal, state, and local prisons or jails for drug offenses; more than 200,000 students lost federal financial aid eligibility because of a drug conviction; and in that same year 43,982 died to an over-dose.[19]

While the government tries to combat the problem the drug culture continues to thrive and gain support from alliance groups like High Times and the DPA. Their solution to the war on drugs is to allow people to use drugs freely and without penalty by regulating the drug culture, but such action will never solve the problem because the

---

[17] www.drugpolicy.org/drug-war-statistics

[18] www.drugpoicy.org/home

[19] www.drugpolicy.org/drug-war-statistics

solution is not to legalize and make available the poison that is destroying people's lives but offer healing that can only come through faith in our Lord Jesus Christ.

The drug culture claims they are advocating for freedom, but Jesus Christ is the only way to real freedom. This is the freedom I now advocate for in response to the drug war. In order to heal the physical body, you must first clean up the heart, from the inside out not the outside in. We can learn from history and the *"Holy Bible"* that there have been times when the people became unruly *"In those days there was no King in Israel. Everyone did what was right in his own eyes"* (Judges 17:6 ESV). Giving in to drug addicts' desires will always yield unsuccessful results. The only way to solve the war on drugs is to provide the hope and healing that they really need.

I was healed of my drug addiction before my dream of going to Amsterdam ever came true. After accepting Christ, the desires of my heart changed and I thank God that instead of visiting Amsterdam, I was able to visit the Holy State of Israel in 2009. After accepting Christ my heart's desires changed. My dreams went from the epitome of Amsterdam to the holiness of Israel. My purpose was sober and focused and my goals had meaning. I quit reading *"High Times"* to read the *"Holy Bible"* and the message found within those pages came alive in my heart and sent me on a journey to the promise land.

## "HOLY BIBLE" and ISRAEL

The "Holy Bible" has become my most prized possession. After looking for my identity in random places, my search ended at the cross of Jesus Christ and led me to the Bible. My road to freedom began once I allowed the authority of the Holy Bible to expose my ugliness and gave God's Word the right to clean me up from the inside out.

I have put faith in a lot of exterior beliefs like evolution, politics, medication, relationships, drugs, magazines, etc... but once I put my faith in God's word I began to develop trust in Him and this helped solve a deep longing to belong. Putting my faith in God's Word solved the inner struggles of evolution, politics, medication, relationships, and drug addiction. There is healing in this book for this life as well as eternity. Being washed in the Word will set you free.

The Holy Bible is God's amazing love letter to you and me told in a collection of 66 books. These books were written over a period of more than 1500 years by more than 40 very different men, some of whom were rich while others were poor. The authors included a priest, a tax collector, a physician, and a few fishermen as well as kings, poets, musicians, philosophers, farmers, and teachers. These men wrote God's Word in many places such as palaces, prisons, great cities, the wilderness, and multiple continents during times of war and times of peace. The Bible contains the creation account, history, prophecy, proverbs, poetry, and letters.

All known facts about God's chosen people, the Israelites, derive from the nation of Israel in the Middle East Region. God chose Israel to set His blessing upon, and this is the land that our Lord and Savior walked with mankind and gave His life a ransom for those who believe in Him. All the promises in God's word were recorded in Israel and when I started reading the "Holy Bible" I began to desire to visit God's holy land.

On July 24, 2009 I was led by the spirit to talk to Clarence Brown, a local Evangelist. Clarence shared with me that he had just returned from a missionary trip to his homeland Kenya, Africa, which he had never visited before.

I was so excited for him because I could see how much joy the trip had brought him. As I listened to him share his experience, I realized his desire to go to Kenya mirrored my desire to go to Israel.

I shared with him how much I dreamed of going to Israel and how I had researched and studied the region. It was clear that Israel had a special place in my heart. He confirmed the same longing with wanting to go to Kenya and described how God made it happen through a miracle.

After we talked, and a little time had passed, I realized the timing of this meeting had been ordained by God. Clarence had just returned from his dream come true while my dream was closer than ever. I remember sharing with Clarence how I had been reacquainted with a high school friend, Todd Browning through Facebook. I had not talked to Todd for over 22 years. Todd and I were basketball teammates in elementary all the way through high school.

It was through this Facebook friend request that I learned Todd was living in Israel. He moved there in 1993 to attend college at Hebrew University and later went on to play professional basketball in Israel. While in Israel, he received a good job and married an Israeli citizen.

After learning this information I wrote him back quickly and expressed to him how much he should cherish moments living in the Holy Land because some people only dream of visiting a place like Israel. His response was that I was welcome to come and visit and stay with him and his wife, Rachael, and he would show me all of Israel. The only thing that was standing between me and my heart's desire was a plane ticket.

I believed that God was at work behind the scenes and that I would soon be on my way to Israel. One week later we had our dear friends, Mark and Tammy Murphy, over for dinner and I told them about my friend and my desire to go to Israel. At that moment, Mark committed to raise the money I needed to fly to Israel.

The first call that Mark made raised $500 for my first mission trip. It was on this night that I received confirmation to begin preparing for my trip to Israel. I began making plans; I had just graduated from OCU-Bedford and was now a student at Liberty University continuing my studies in Theology.

The fundraising was completed on August 6th and school started on August 24th. For this trip to happen, it would only be an act of God. I was able to book a flight out on the 10th and return on the 25th. That gave me less than 14 days to explore Israel.

I cannot fully describe the excitement and anticipation I felt once I arrived in Israel. I wanted to grow in several areas of my life, gain a better understanding of God's word, and return home a better man, husband, and father. I also hoped to receive insight and revelation for my purpose on Earth in God's Kingdom. I believed that this trip was God's way of bringing the *"Holy Bible"* to life in a powerful way. I remember asking God to keep my mind focused on the leading of the Holy Spirit.

My journey to Israel was unlike most tourists, Christians, and religious observers because I didn't have a paid tour guide or a daily itinerary, but rather, I was on an independent tour of the Holy Land led by the Holy Spirit and an old friend who had a house in a small town called Kfar Saba.

Todd had to work during most of my visit so he did his best to show me the bus routes and help me develop a plan for each day's journey. There were many days we toured together to the more dangerous and remote locations of Israel. One great thing about this trip was that I felt safe while riding on the buses that are often targets of suicide bombers, even though Israeli soldiers sitting next to me had their weapons lying across their lap. The presence of the military brought a sense of peace not fear.

One stop that I particularly enjoyed was the Wailing Wall. In Jerusalem, people come from all over the world to write their prayer requests on a piece of paper and place them in a crack in the Wailing Wall. The Wailing Wall is basically a retaining wall that holds back fill dirt and stones so that the temple can be erected on level ground. This is the oldest remaining section of the old Temple in Jerusalem and people come from all over the world to pray at what is considered the Holiest place on earth.

Excitement overwhelmed me as I approached this historical wall with my prayer request in hand. Every stone was carefully placed one on another by our forefathers, prophets, and servants of God. I was literally surrounded by a great cloud of witnesses inside the city walls of Jerusalem. As I got closer, I expressed my thoughts through the leading of the Holy Spirit, *"At this moment I approach this wall to place my paper of prayers, I feel God's presence, this is special and it is a great blessing to be here. But, the same God I am coming to pray to is the same God I pray to and have a personal relationship with everywhere I go, He goes with me..."*

I was so blessed to be reminded that religion and sacrifice is worthless without love and mercy. I was called to live in a relationship with God wherever His Spirit leads and to walk in obedience to His purpose for my life wherever I am.

While I visited in Jerusalem I was blessed to tour the city and get a personal feel for the Jewish and Palestinian culture. The most memorable landmark was what most Christians believe to be the Garden of Joseph of Arimathea and what took place in its vicinity. I looked death in the eyes at the *"place of the skull,"* the hill where our Savior bled and died.

In the same hour, I walked into the tomb where we believe Christ was raised from the dead. My faith grew immensely in that moment, standing where Jesus was resurrected. God could have sent many other people on this journey, but he chose me to go even though I was an ex-felon and ex-convict with a reckless past of deceit and manipulation. That was a humbling experience I will never forget.

The Bible came to life as I recognized names and locations through street signs. I would flip through my Bible as I traveled by bus or vehicle to read about the Biblical accounts that happened at different locations. Traveling through the Valley of Megiddo led me to Revelations and the Armageddon. Being in Shiloh led me to the 369 years the tabernacle rested. As I drove through the terrain of Nazareth I understood why the disciple said *"no good thing comes from Nazareth."* The property and landscape was torrential.

This opportunity to visit such diverse scenery was a once- in-a lifetime event. After walking through the Yad Vashem museum that houses miles of Jewish history demonstrating how they have been mistreated and put to death throughout history, I was personally moved and I will forever carry Israel and the Jewish people in a special place in my heart.

Touring the landscape of Israel was phenomenal, driving through miles and miles of Dessert and Valleys of Israel and the sudden appearance of the Wadi David where David fled and Saul pursued was remarkable. Coming over the crest and catching my first glimpse of the Sea of Galilee will never be forgotten.

I also had some time for leisure. There are five bodies of water in Israel and I was blessed to have the opportunity to swim in four of them. I visited Netanya on the Mediterranean Coast which is known for *"Great beaches in Israel"* for a day of family fun. I spent the day with Todd and all of Rachael's Israeli family eating fresh fruit and playing paddle ball with a couple of Israeli boys.

When I visited the Jordan River I first went to the visitor's center at the mouth of the Sea of Galilee. This is where they perform baptisms for a fee and people come from all over the world to be baptized close to the same place Jesus was baptized. I had already been baptized more than once. Once at eight years old into the Mormon Church and once in a baby pool in an isolation cell we called the drunk tank at Lawrence County Jail. And finally, I was baptized because I believed in my heart and made Jesus Lord of my life after I received Salvation at *"Organics Plus"* in 2005.

Being at the river where Jesus was baptized and where great men of God come from all over the world to perform baptisms, I was faced with an interesting proposition. Wouldn't it be great to be baptized in the Jordan River? Yes, that would be incredible; however, I had already been baptized and I was already a son of God. I decided that as religious of an experience as that would be I would go swimming instead.

We left the visitors center and freelanced down the river onto the property of a Kibbutz. A Kibbutzim is a gathering or cluster of people who choose to live together in community. This particular Kibbutz reminded me more of a liberal, hippy commune than a religious Monastic community. Nevertheless, I was free to experience the thrill of swimming in the Jordan River. It was such a great time that I looked forward to swimming in the Sea of Galilee later that same afternoon.

I had experienced some low times in my life before Christ, and as a matter of fact, I eventually hit rock bottom. I did a lot of people wrong and some things I did to others were disgusting. I have been at the bottom but I have never been as low on the earth as I was the day I floated in the Dead Sea. The Dead Sea is the lowest place on the planet and it was beautiful to see how God brings us up and out of a dead life and into a resurrected life in Him.

I was not able to make it to the Red Sea to visit and swim but I pray if the Lord allows that one day I shall return. And I am going to cross over that body of water as I reflect on the great Exodus from Egypt and how God offers us deliverance from the world through acceptance of Jesus Christ as our Lord.

Even though it was a great experience to swim in the waters we read about in the Holy Bible, the greatest pool of water for me is still the baptismal water made ready for a converted soul to publically confess their new found faith and resurrected life in Christ, wherever that may be. God promises that *"Therefore, If anyone is in Christ, he is a new creation. The old has passed away; behold, the new has come"* (2 Corinthians 5:17 ESV). Seeing a new Christian wash away their old lifestyle in the living water of our Lord Jesus Christ is incredible every time.

When we become new creatures through God's living water, His desires for our life become our desires. Many people misunderstand when they hear this scripture *"Take delight in the Lord, and He will give you the desires of your heart"* (Psalm 37:4 NIV). God doesn't give us our desires without us first delighting in Him. If that had been the case he would have given me the desire to go to Amsterdam, but once I began to delight in Him, my desires were altered and ultimately His desires and His promises came true.

In addition to changes in my desire I also quit responding to the call of 420 and instead responded to Jesus's call from Matthew 4:20. Jesus' call to his disciples to follow him is still the same for us today. We are here to make disciples according to the Bible not culture. Our war today is not with flesh and blood but the deception that has invaded our culture and church's. We are not at war with drugs, high times, or sinners. We are at war with SIN and the root cause of the sin problem.

By writing these words, I hope to rid a culture of a despicable slogan by rooting out, pulling down, and destroying its appeal and offer something new that we can begin to build and plant. In *"High Times"* and the drug culture 4:20 means *"Let's get High."* In the *"Holy Bible"* Matthew 4:20 is a response by a true disciple of Jesus Christ, one that is willing to walk away from everything to follow the one whose calling is worthy.

After I arrived home from Israel I began to serve in recovery support for the next two years while I finished up my studies at Liberty University. In 2011 we received the property in the Guthrie bottoms that the Lord had promised us for 4 years. We answered the call to disciple men for God while being called back home.

After being reconciled to Christ many of us run away from our home towns because running is what we have always done. I ran from my past for several years, but God's calling on my life was to come back home. Home is where I needed to be for God.

# -7-

# From Home to Home

## *Oh heart of mine, come back home*

*"You will know the truth, and the truth will set you free."*

John 8:32 ESV

God has given each of us a unique place on this earth that we can call home. This is usually the place where we were raised. But at some point we must choose our home according to God's purpose for our own life. For some, that means continuing to serve where they started, in the place they have always called home. For others, that may mean serving in a completely new location away from their hometown.

For me, God has called me right back to the place I have always considered home – Guthrie Bottoms. This is where my mother and father bought land, built a house and chose to raise a family. Throughout my childhood in Guthrie Bottoms, I was taught Mormon doctrines, told to confess that Joseph Smith was a prophet of God, and that the Church of Jesus Christ of Latter Day Saints is the only true church. It was in Guthrie Bottoms that I also chose to leave the fellowship of the Mormon Church at age 14. And at the age of 17, I chose to leave the place I had always known as home. Once I left home I was told, *"You will be back; those that leave the church always come back home."*

When I left home for the first time, I had no idea what I was looking for. I only knew there was emptiness deep in my heart that needed to be filled, so for the next 20 years I attempted to fill that void with anything and everything that brought me relief and pleasure. During that time, I realized the searching was of little worth, though, because nothing I did took away the empty feeling.

I went through several different phases over this twenty-year period. I married, landed a good paying job, bought land, moved a trailer onto the property, and called this home for a short time. When this didn't satisfy me, I got divorced and experimented with a new home as a single guy living in a party-life atmosphere. When I tired of that, I decided the married life was better so I found me another wife and attempted to buy land and a home, but at that point, the hole in my heart was too dark. I lived in trashy trailer parks and roach infested motels. I slept in dirty beds with dirty clothes. On the other hand, I also experienced what it was like to have money, nice things, and enjoy luxury vacations.

I attempted to fill the emptiness in my heart by creating different places to call home and feel at peace. The problem with this strategy, and why I was unsuccessful, is that I was doing it on my own instead of allowing God to show me His purpose for my life and lead me home.

As I have shared with you, I completely surrendered to God and his purpose in 2005. After I gave up my old way of living to follow Christ, my family assumed I would come back home to the church I grew up in. The Mormon Church, its missionaries, and my mother were convinced that my leaving the church was why my life became such a wreck. Since I cleaned up my life, they felt it was time for me to return to the Mormon faith and greatly pressured me to do so.

At the same time, my new friends in the Christian faith counseled me to build a new life completely away from my hometown to stay clear of any temptation from my old way of living.

Even though I was pressured in two different directions by my Mormon family and Christian friends, everyone agreed that I couldn't lead a successful life in Bedford, IN if I continued on the path I had been taking. With good reason, they were concerned I wouldn't be able to stand against the temptations of my past decisions and failures nor the influence of old friends. In addition, being an ex-felon and ex-convict was something everyone thought would hinder me from finding employment locally. People were pressuring me to go where I could be the most successful, but leading a successful life and leading a purposeful life are two different things.

When I thought about both arguments presented to me, I realized I wanted truth more than anything else. My view of God, Christ, and truth never lined up with the Mormon teachings, so I knew if I went back to my hometown, I definitely couldn't return to the Mormon Church.

On the other hand, even though it seemed challenging to move back and be successful in the same place my life fell apart, I wanted to discover purpose because I believed that was the key to living a meaningful life with an eternal impact rather than earthly success that is temporary. Finding my purpose in Christ ultimately led me back to my hometown, and it is this purpose in Christ that allowed me to discover freedom.

Because I was desperately seeking a life of purpose, I prayed for God's guidance to lead me. He answered my prayer and showed me purpose by bringing me back home to the same neighborhood I was raised as a Mormon and rebellious drug dealer. Although I have returned home to the Guthrie Bottoms, nothing in my current life resembles my past life.

This time, I returned home a new creature in Jesus Christ. I am not alone because I have the Word of God living in me. I am free from Mormonism and have found purpose for my life. With God's direction for my purpose and mission for my time here on earth, I find comfort and peace in the place I call home. The same is true for you, so wherever God calls you to serve, that will be home, and you will know you are at home when you find that same comfort and peace that I have found.

## HOME ON EARTH

When we refer to our earthly home, we often think of the phrase, *"There's no place like home."* And it is true, there really is no other place where you can feel comfortable and relax. It is the place where you can be yourself, in your truest form without fancy clothes or make-up or the need to impress anyone. You can relax, put your hair on the dresser, put your teeth in a cup, and have one sock on and one sock off. Home is your domain. You can rest in the comfort of your home.

As Christians, our earthly home is more than a geographical location. We must also be home in the spirit, which happens when we lead a purposeful life where we do not have to pretend to be something we are not because we know we have been fearfully and wonderfully made with unique skills, talents, and abilities. Where we don't have to compete with anybody or try to impress because we are using what God gave us to glorify and please him alone. Where we minister effectively and appreciate everyone's unique gifts as one body of Christ fulfilling the great commission to save those who are lost. One of the greatest signs of being *"Free at Last"* is God leads you home here on earth and eternally in Heaven.

God wants us to be free and that is His purpose in leading us home. We need to be at home on this earth because it keeps us in the presence of Jesus. God doesn't need anything but he wants us to need him as scripture says, *"He did this so they might seek God, and perhaps they might reach out and find Him, though He is not far from each one of us"* (Acts 17:27 ESV). As Christians, Earth is just our temporary home. Heaven is our eternal home and while we are here on Earth, we are just preparing for our eternal home that God created for His glory out of love.

There is a long road and a short road to home. The long road is hard and full of trouble, and we go through it more or less blind and deceived. But there is also a short road home where we can see the path and know we are accomplishing our purpose here on earth. I am a slow learner, and I took the long and hard way home. It didn't have to be this way but it was the path I chose to take. You don't have to take the long and hard way home. But if you already are on that road, there is still hope for you through Jesus Christ.

That is the beautiful thing that has come out of a life that I should not have survived. I have been strengthened by Christ to testify and share my failures with many that are like me; this is my purpose while I am on earth.

If you are a Christian, you can often look back at your journey and see how God works in mysterious and sometimes ironic ways. As I look back, I think it is quite humorous how the beginning of my rebellion was in the Guthrie Bottoms. It is amazing that when I was a boy the Pastor of the Church grounds where we now live use to run me off the property for mischievous behavior. I thank God for a man that rebuked me when I was a rebellious young man. I would guess the last thing that Pastor ever thought was that I would be the future Pastor that would live in his house, sleep in his bedroom, and preach in his pulpit.

In order to continue on with my purpose here in Guthrie Bottoms, I must humbly accept one major restriction for my life and that is I can't go back into death, rebellion, criminal behavior, or a false religion. The good news is God has given me the tools needed to stay strong in following Him. The Lord has provided an environment and Christian family that makes it possible to live life as a disciple of Christ. God has strengthened me by allowing me to offer to others the things that were missing in my life. As I raise my son and future disciples, I use a lot of experiences from my past to help them on their journey to freedom in Christ.

For instance, I have recognized that discipleship was missing in my life. I never had a Godly man that walked with me through life's joys and sorrows. I understand now that my father losing his father at age 13 created an absence in his life that left him unable to know how to be a father that communicated with a son. I resented him growing up as a teenager, but today I look at it from a whole new perspective. And it makes sense today that God has used this void to give me a desire to be a disciple maker, mentor, father, coach, and teacher to my son and men like me. They need guidance as I did.

It is for this reason today that I keep a watchful eye on my son and the students God entrusts me with. I have chosen to develop my son's God given abilities and talents at a moderate pace. I talk to him, I invest in him and he has chosen to put confidence in my leadership. We have developed goals and disciplines with patience and priorities that will develop him spiritually, physically, and mentally.

Training a child in the way he should go is more than pounding the Bible into them. I didn't have the upbringing my son or the men I disciple are receiving because I had no one take me under their wing and guide me through these difficult years. No matter what my son or the students at HNHC choose to become, they will be prepared to face success and failure in this life. To make disciples of all nations is my first and foremost commitment to the Lord as a husband, father, teacher, mentor, coach, and any other role I am given while here on earth.

Another thing from my past that has become a huge blessing to the ministry is that I have learned how to grow a garden God's way. In the old life, I was driven to grow marijuana to support a habit and as a way of financial stability. Today, we cultivate a garden every year that produces a great deal of produce. The students help and we teach them how to can and preserve in various ways. We make a special jalapeno pepper relish that has had nothing but grand reviews. We make our own salsa, pickles, and relish. It is a great joy to see men walk through the seedling stage to the harvest stage. I never thought I would see our students leaving with the desire to garden when they get their own piece of ground. God took an old pot grower and used his talents to grow gardens God's way.

One of the challenges of living a life of purpose that Christians must be aware of is becoming so spiritual that we are of no earthly good. This happens when we become self-righteous, forgetting the mercy God shows us, and lacking mercy towards others. That is why it is important to know that God's calling for you first and foremost on this earth is to make disciples. Once you discover this and live it whole-heartedly, there is nothing more freeing than to know you are right where God wants you to be.

## HOME IN HEAVEN

Heaven Nevaeh Healing Center started with a passion to help men realize that there is more to live for than what this world has to offer. I want to share with you why the ministry is named Heaven Nevaeh.

Heaven has to be a real place. Despite fallacies about reclining on clouds and playing harps, we won't be sitting and doing nothing in heaven. We will rest, but this holy relief is from all the things that make life on earth so wearying—temptation, trials, heartache, and pain. Scripture refers to our future hope in this way, *and I heard a voice from heaven saying, "Write this: Blessed are the dead who die in the Lord from now on." "Blessed indeed," says the Spirit, that they may rest from their labors, for their deeds follow them"* (Revelations 14:13 ESV). Heaven is a real place that we receive by faith which is *"confidence in what we hope for and assurance about what we do not see"* (Hebrews 11:1 NIV).

The Bible states that we can live in Heaven for eternity with Jesus, *"But in keeping with his promise, we are looking forward to a new heaven and a new earth, where righteousness dwells"* (2 Peter 3:13 ESV). Paradise is beyond our imagination, but we do know that the believer's life goes on in heaven. As citizens of that realm, we will take up the work of serving and praising God. Moreover, we will enjoy unlimited energy and perfect harmony between the Lord, ourselves, and other saints.

This is what we want our students to understand—that Heaven is for real—our ultimate home—and our earthly goal. We live this life for the life to come by keeping our focus on things that are above because the Bible commands, *"Set your minds on things that are above, not on things that are on the earth"* (Colossians 3:2 ESV).

Nevaeh is the word Heaven turned around which represents the turning point through our Lord Jesus Christ. When a person is sick and tired of being at the bottom or running into the same stone wall, the only options are to look up or turn around and go a different direction. We all have to change our thinking and our old way of life for heaven to become a real place. HNHC is a faith-based discipleship program for those who have made the first step to overcoming their trials and turning their lives around by accepting Jesus Christ as their personal Savior.

We are now in the year 2015 of our Lord Jesus Christ and HNHC has been in operation for $3^{1/2}$ years. I want to share some statistics to demonstrate how God can work through the obedience and the ministry of one person that is willing to reach one person at a time. I hope this progress inspires you to take time to minister to the people in your life as well. It is our goal to see men fall in love with Jesus and His Word. We believe that if this happens they will change.

These statistics have been accumulated from October 27, 2011 through May 16, 2015

> 103 men have been accepted into housing at HNHC
>
> 38 of these men have left upon completion of their requirements
>
> 5,798 beds have been provided to men seeking help

17,394 individual meals have been served

16,801 man hours of community service have been provided by HNHC

23,851 hours have been spent in the Word (Bible studies, chapel, outside services)

50,793 printed pages of Biblical Studies

Perhaps the most moving picture of the impact of Heaven Nevaeh is a success story. The following are just a few examples of changed lives through HNHC.

## David Sheldon

David was our very first student at HNHC (Now FAL) in 2011. He came to us as a Heroin addict from Kinston, Washington. David completed the program and fell in love with Jesus. He is now serving as a Sunday school teacher at Crossroads Community Church in Bedford, Indiana with his wife, Kendal, who grew up in the church. David continues to serve at HNHC to help others like him find freedom in Christ and he is beginning the process of starting his own 501(c) 3 ministry, Latter Glory House, to assist new brothers making the transition back into everyday life.

*David & Kendal Sheldon 2015*

# Jonpaul Pool

Jonpaul, was a lover of darkness, self, and sin before coming to know the power of the Holy Spirit. He was addicted to heroin, methadone, and methamphetamines. Jonpaul lost everything including his relationship with his two boys. By the Grace of God, which brings salvation, appeared to him; this alone taught Jonpaul how to say NO to ungodliness, worldly passions, and showed him how to live an upright life for JESUS. Since leaving the ministry he met a young lady by the name of Amber. Amber was a school teacher at a Christian School for children. God truly sent Amber to help him live out his Christian life. They were married and are currently pursuing their foster care license. They also do ministry through Community Care Network and Living Streams Community Church. Amber is a school teacher and Jonpaul is an electrician that looks forward to teaching the youth in their home Church.

*Jonpaul & Amber Pool 2021*

## Mark Butler

Mark is from Brownstown, Indiana and was a major Heroin and Meth addict until he fell in love with Jesus. Upon completion of HNHC in-house discipleship program in 2013, Mark joined some friends of ours in Sabetha, Kansas. He is now living with two police officers and works for KSI Conveyors as a lead service technician.

*Mark Butler 2015*

At HNHC, we believe it is our purpose and mission to prepare our students for their journey home in heaven and to tell them about Jesus so they can go and tell others about Jesus. That journey all begins with the ultimate question in life; the question my students and I all had to face to find freedom. It is a question that will change your life forever if you are ready and willing to answer it.

131

Now, I seize the opportunity to ask you this most important question – Are you ready to come home on earth and in heaven? Are you ready to spend your time now and for eternity with Jesus?

I pray as you read the final chapter, your heart yearns to answer and respond to this call on your life.

# -8-

# Are You Ready to Come Home?

## *My Heart for You*

*"You also be ready, for the Son of Man is coming at an hour you do not expect."*

Luke 12:40 ESV

On June 07, 2014 we were saddened when a brother from the ministry went home to be with the Lord. Even though the Bible tells us *"a good name is better than fine perfume, and the day of death better than the day of birth"* (Ecclesiastes 7:1 NIV), we still struggle with accepting heaven as a real place when we lose a loved one. I want to share the testimony of my brother in the Lord, Brandon Stiles.

I remember the first time I met Brandon. He pulled into the parking lot of the ministry with his mother. The brothers and I were laying foundation block for our new wood building. After a brief introduction, he asked me what he had to do to come to Heaven Nevaeh. I asked him if he was sick of it and if he wanted to change. When he said yes, I told him to get his stuff and come right back.

Brandon was a man of few words and it was obvious from the beginning that he was a man on a mission. He chose his words carefully, and he observed what was going on out of sheer desire to change. He would be the first to say that his seven months at HNHC weren't easy, but they were worth it.

One day in his first week at HNHC, he got up during morning Bible studies and was going to quit. As he reached the door he saw a picture of Jesus with these words, *"I never said it would be easy, just worth it,"* and he turned around and sat back down.

Brandon came in with a heart condition called cardiomyopathy, an acquired or hereditary disease of the heart muscle that makes it hard for the heart to deliver blood to the body. It could have been caused by his habitual drug abuse but whatever the reason, the Lord had allowed it. I believe Brandon knew something we all didn't. He was going to die and he had to choose life or death. He could die and go to heaven or he could die and go to hell. He chose to listen to the words of God and that decision radically changed his life.

The night Brandon received Christ at the altar, I knew the moment our eyes met we were now blood brothers. Very few times have I witnessed this kind of transformation. A man on a mission is oftentimes a man of few words. The task at hand was Brandon's focus. The way he saw it, he had been talking his whole life; it was time to be a doer. Brandon decided he would live the rest of his life putting God first and others second.

Brandon came here clueless about God and the Church. He had been a major drug dealer since his early years of high school. He didn't go into much detail about his illegal activity, but I know of a few instances where people actually lost their lives. Whether Brandon handled the gun I don't know, but I do know he wasn't proud of what he had been involved in. I believe that is because God got a hold of his spiritual heart and would not let go.

We really thought God would heal Brandon's heart condition. He went through each day like nothing was wrong. As we went forward we had no idea his death would come so soon, but the Lord knew it all along.

I have talked about Jesus and the Bible being enough in people's life. Another reason why this is so important was lived out in

Brandon's life. On the last day Brandon was with us, he didn't have any great doctrinal revelations. He had a normal day of working in the yard, gardening, and planning a cookout with his boys for the following night. He was content, prepared, and ready to go home.

God had prepared Brandon for his eternal call home. Brandon didn't have a religious experience with a bunch of bells and whistles. Brandon Stiles met Jesus and let Jesus change him. He died doing what he loved — serving others. He spent his last days as the orphans and widows minister at Mt. Pleasant Christian Church. God restored his marriage and his wife's faith in Christ. Brandon is still leaving a mark on this community and ministry, and heaven is a better place because Brandon has come home.

*Brandon & Amanda Stiles with the kids,*
*Coleson, Case, and Caylee 2015*

We never know what we truly believe until it's a matter of life and death. The sad thing is that we have really not lived until we have received Christ as our personal Lord and Savior. The greatest hope I can have on this planet is to know Jesus as Lord and have heaven to look forward to for all eternity.

The bible says that *"faith is sure of what we hope for and certain of what we do not see"* (Hebrews 11:1 NIV). Will you receive by faith what you do not deserve and come home to the one who knows you better than anyone else?

I want all those who have read this book to know that there is not one question more important than this: Are you ready to come home to Jesus? Who better is there to encourage us than the message that Billy Graham committed his life to.

> [Of all the things I've seen and heard there is only one message that can change people's lives and hearts. I want to tell people about the meaning of the cross. Not the cross that hangs on the wall or around someone's neck, but the real cross of Christ. It's sacred and blood stained, his is a rugged cross, though many will react to this message, it is the truth and I want to leave you with the truth...He loves you and He is willing to forgive you of your sins...God wants you to live and he wants you to live life to the fullest and he has a plan for you that will prosper you and bless you, Jesus said, I have come that they might have life-life in all its fullness...to give you the assurance that your sin is forgiven and that you are going to heaven when you die] [20]

Billy Graham

There is no other way to Heaven unless one comes through the cross. If my hope is to be in heaven, then I have put my hope in the cross and what was accomplished on the cross for all who wish to be saved. The cross does not suggest, it demands a new lifestyle. God can make you into a whole new person.

---

[20] www.myhopewithbillygraham.org; @2013 Billy Graham Evangelistic Association

Do you not know you have been bought with a price? The love that God displayed through the brutal crucifixion of His own son shows us how badly God desired to redeem us and save us from an eternity in hell. This is why I have hope in Jesus. This is why I have hope in heaven. The promises of God are true, and I believe because I have witnessed his display of love in my own life. If God loved me so much that he reached down and rescued me from all my failures, then I have to believe he will also bring me to be with Him one day in paradise.

The truth is there is no other way to be free. Jesus is the way to the Father

[Thomas said to him, "Lord, we don't know where you are going, so how can we know the way?" Jesus answered, "I am the way and the truth and the life. No one comes to the Father except through me. If you really know me, you will know my Father as well. From now on, you do know him and have seen him.]

John 14:5-7 NIV

Christ took the hell you and I deserve. I am free because Christ came and rescued me. If you want to be free, receive it, believe in it, and put your trust in Christ. If you come to the cross of Christ broken and humble, you will experience your own disciple's journey, and you too my friend will experience the life of being *"Free at Last."*

# Contact Info:

## Got Purpose?
We Help__On a Mission from God!
www.freeatlast777.com
YOUR JOURNEY_A PLACE TO BELONG

**David Louis Norris Jr.**

Email:  support@freeatlast777.com

## Free at Last Ministries
67 Valley Mission L
Bedford, IN  47421

Phone:  812-583-8115

**Website:**

**www.freeatlast777.com**

Made in the USA
Columbia, SC
20 June 2022

61854977R00076